16-95 ✓

of related interest

The Essential Groupworker
Teaching and Learning Creative Groupwork
Mark Doel and Catherine Sawdon
ISBN 1 85302 823 1

Taking the Group Seriously
Towards a Post-Foulkesian Group Analytic Theory
Farhad Dalal
ISBN 1 85302 642 5
International Library of Group Analysis 5

Autobiography of a Theory
Developing a Systems-Centred Theory
Yvonne M. Agazarian and Susan P. Gantt
ISBN 1 85302 847 9

Creative Group Therapy for Women Survivors of Child Sexual Abuse
Speaking the Unspeakable
Bonnie Meekums
ISBN 1 85302 543 8

The Group Context
Sheila Thompson
ISBN 1 85302 657 3
International Library of Group Analysis 7

Active Analytic Group Therapy for Adolescents
John Evans
ISBN 1 85302 616 6 pb
ISBN 1 85302 615 8 hb

Competence in Social Work Practice
Edited by Kieran O'Hagan
ISBN 1 85302 332 9

Handbook of Theory for Practice Teachers in Social Work
Edited by Joyce Lishman
ISBN 1 85302 098 2

Creative Training
Sociodrama and Team-building
Ron Wiener
ISBN 1 85302 422 8

Practice Teaching – Changing Social Work
Edited by Hilary Lawson
ISBN 1 85302 478 3

Choosing a Groupwork Approach

An Inclusive Stance

Oded Manor

Jessica Kingsley Publishers
London and Philadelphia

The right of Oded Manor to be identified as author of this work has been asserted by him in accordance with the Copyright, Designs and Patents Act 1988.

First published in the United Kingdom in 2000 by
Jessica Kingsley Publishers Ltd,
116 Pentonville Road, London
N1 9JB, England
and
325 Chestnut Street,
Philadelphia PA 19106, USA.

www.jkp.com

© Copyright 2000 Oded Manor

Library of Congress Cataloging in Publication Data
A CIP catalog record for this book is available from the Library of Congress

British Library Cataloguing in Publication Data
A CIP catalogue record for this book is available from the British Library

ISBN 1 85302 870 3

Printed and Bound in Great Britain by
Athenaeum Press, Gateshead, Tyne and Wear

Contents

Acknowledgements

Many people have contributed helpful suggestions while I have been preparing this book. I cannot list all of them but I would like to thank particularly Tom Douglas, Charles Garvin, and Charlotte Heath.

This book is dedicated to Illi, my mother,
who understands so much about what it
means to choose with love

Introduction

How do you actually work with each group? A model to help you choose will be developed in this book. Right now, you may well ask: why yet another model? Do we not have too many of them already? Indeed we do, but this creative diversity also leads to a problem.

At present, groupwork is offered by professionals in many different disciplines: occupational therapy or community development, social work or psychiatric nursing, youth work or health promotion, criminal justice or various forms of education. People of all age groups are offered groupwork to meet very diverse needs: education, personal growth, mutual aid, and social change are only four of the goals pursued in these groups.

In addition, groupwork practice thrives within different institutions such as residential care and schools and hospitals, as well as in the open community. Indeed, whenever help with feelings, thoughts and practical needs are combined, groupwork can be identified as a viable form of intervention.

Not only are practice settings diverse, but the range of clients' needs are immensely broad. Practitioners resort to many different explanations when they account for their practice – from cognitive-behavioural, through psychodynamic, to humanistic methods.

Why is this a problem?

With so many forms of groupwork available, it is virtually impossible for groups to be compared and contrasted. As a result, it is not always clear that workers choose the groupwork approach that may best meet their clients' needs. Such fragmentation also prevents groupworkers from building up groupwork knowledge so that the practice can improve.

Yet, each form of groupwork may have its own merit. This is why the present inclusive stance does not reject any existing practice. Instead, a model for evolving many different groupwork models is offered. This model is a 'three-cornered world' that can include very different practices. Within this triangular framework, each worker may be able to explain the groupwork approach chosen and show how it is similar to and different from the approaches chosen by others. More specifically, this three-cornered world may help in at least five areas:

Being purposeful

The model will help you identify the specific stages of group development most relevant to meeting group members' needs. With these stages in mind, you may be able to focus on your involvement more effectively, and so more easily pursue the purpose of the group.

Identifying outcomes

When you have a clearer understanding as to how the purpose of the group can be served during each groupwork stage, you may find it easier to see what group members gain from each of these periods. You may then be in a position to explain which gains build up to form the outcomes of members' involvement in this particular group.

Clarifying what you do

The detailed analysis of group stages and the forms of worker involvement in each can enable you to explain what you do. Many may want to know this; for example, members of the group, your supervisor, and your manager. One of the ways of strengthening commitment to, and support of, groupwork is by making it transparent to those not involved in direct groupwork practice. For this, a shared language is needed. Indeed, the present framework explains groupwork as grounded in the systems approach. Among other advantages, this approach is also one which is used by many practitioners in various other fields in the helping professions. Therefore, your practice may more easily make sense to others.

Building up your knowledge

Let us take an example: working with one group of adolescents you may have chosen an educational approach, as the purpose was to inform the youngsters about safe sex. Next, you are asked to work with an adolescent group where they can explore sexual relationships. Hopefully, you will not offer both groups the same approach, but you will not start from scratch either. Taking the inclusive stance, you will be able to identify the aspects that you may borrow from sex education groups and draw on these while working with the new group. But more may well be needed. So, you may then add to the aspects you already know new ones – those that are needed in a group about sexual relationships. Once you have worked with one group, you can use the experience to more accurately choose how to work with quite a different one.

Finding out more

The inclusive stance adopted here may enable each worker to separate his/her own practice from that of others, while also connecting it to other forms of groupwork practice; ones that different groupwork practitioners follow. Such cross-fertilisation can help systematic research of groupwork, and so – the inclusive stance may help in advancing groupwork knowledge and improving groupwork practice.

This book is an attempt to propose a framework that has evolved out of a certain understanding of the systems approach. Perhaps not surprisingly, it took several years to develop this framework. During that period various versions of the manuscript have been read by quite a number of leading groupworkers in the world. It occurs to me that perhaps I can introduce this book by responding to the helpful questions that have arisen.

What is the problem?

The problem of choosing a groupwork approach has to be broken down into a number of questions.

The immense diversity in groupwork practice is not necessarily a problem. Over the three decades of being involved in groupwork, my own practice has embraced many different theories and disparate techniques. As that range widened, I began to realise I had a problem: other people were saying that I was 'jumping' from one model to another in what appeared to them as a haphazard way. Yet, when I began to explain my thinking it appeared that I was not chopping and changing arbitrarily. Those conversations were useful: in the process I began to wonder if I was the only groupworker who suffered from this problem. Fortunately, I was also involved as a groupwork consultant, teacher, researcher, and latterly, as the editor of the journal *Groupwork*. These contacts with other groupworkers reassured me. It appeared that the way in which I was involved in expanding the range of my responses might reflect the struggle of other practitioners too. I shall begin with the ways the problem tends to show up.

When workers are asked to describe how they work with a group they often refer to 'the beginning', 'the middle', and 'the end'. Usually it is possible to surmise what may be expected at the beginning and at the end of each group; these stages are relatively clear. Yet, often it is 'the middle' that gives rise to problems. Accounts of the middle period are often rather baffling.

Explanations for the middle period are often offered in relation to one established scheme of group stages. Indeed, experiences in groups are expected to converge around certain themes; such as trust, power, intimacy, or separation, which we call 'stages'. The importance of 'stages' is now very widely accepted. The question that always needs a new answer is which stages appear in which group, and why.

In answering this question, rather puzzling solutions are often attempted. A clear example is the way the scheme of group stages developed by Tuckman and Jensen (1977) may be used.

Many workers know the sequence of forming, norming, storming, performing, and adjourning. The immense contribution of Tuckman and Jensen (1977) sprang from studying T-Groups. 'Training Groups', to restore their original title, were set up for professionals who were invited to learn what happened in a rather unusual situation. That situation involved the professionals meeting together without being given any topic for discussion. The only topic was the experiences happening among them, and between them and the appointed leader. Such direct experiential learning is of immense value.

Yet, closer examination of current practice accounts is often rather perplexing. In these accounts Tuckman and Jensen's (1977) terms are used very liberally. When the details are explored, it appears that all groups do go through the stage of 'forming', but not all really go through 'storming', only some really experience 'norming', and the meaning of 'performing' is often rather vague. Sometimes it is not clear how the group 'adjourned'. Reading such accounts, one may be forgiven for imagining that rhyming is possibly more important than direct and specific descriptions of what happens in each group.

In general, many accounts of groupwork practice are of working with different groups with different purposes. Still, many practitioners seem to expect the same stages to appear in these groups. No wonder, it is often virtually impossible to know whether a worker is as helpful as possible, while working with a particular group.

Why focus on group stages?

Is the solution to abandon group stages? I suggest it is not, as group stages are very helpful signposts. Group stages alert the practitioner to possible ways of focusing on what really matters to most group members, while members develop relationships with the worker and with one another. Abandoning the study of group stages amounts to embarking on a journey into an unknown territory of group relationships without even the most general map in hand. It is true that each group is unique in some ways and never exactly the same as any other group, but not totally unique. Over and above the differences, some commonalities often surface. The territory of each group is special to that group, but often the overall map can be identified in advance. Abandoning the idea of group stages is akin to embarking on a journey, without first identifying some of the major signposts that may well help us in steering our way towards a desirable destination.

Which stages are relevant?

Perhaps the solution is of a different kind. Perhaps it is time to revise the approach we have adopted when exploring group stages. Current approaches to group stages are either pragmatic or fully prescribed. The pragmatic stance can be most clearly associated with the terms 'beginning, middle, and end'. As was suggested, such shorthand pragmatism leaves the middle period rather grossly defined and poorly explained. The fully prescribed stance is very different. This stance involves practitioners in adhering to a ready-made scheme of group stages; such as that developed by Tuckman and Jensen (1977), regardless of the purpose and the context of the group with which they work. Ironically, the result is often the same. Within the prescribed stance, the same terms are used to account for very different groups, and so – the accounts often appear quite unclear and rather unconvincing.

In this book, a third stance towards group stages will be taken. I shall call this 'the evolving stance'. The *evolving stance* is different from the other two in at least three ways.

First, group stages will be defined in greater detail than is usually the case. The stages will be seen as referring not only to the themes that pre-occupy group members. The stages will also include the levels: either personal, interpersonal or social, and the processes of change that may be relevant to each stage.

Second, apart from the beginning and the end, no stage will be prescribed for any group, but a common pool of stages will be identified. This common pool will be called *'the inclusive blueprint'* of group stages, and will be relevant to all forms of groupwork. From that blueprint, each worker will be invited to identify the stages that may be relevant to the particular group with which that worker is involved.

Third, the inclusive blueprint will not be derived from a theory that accounts for any specific and therefore partial need: neither insight into group dynamics, nor emotional growth and development, nor even the need to build up group cohesion will guide the inclusive blueprint, although all may be associated with this framework. The inclusive blueprint will be derived from one overall motive; a need shared by all human beings: that is, the attempt to *communicate* with other human beings. In addition, the inclusive blueprint will be drawn from one feature shared by all those involved in groupwork. This additional aspect is the intention to become aware of what happens in groups. Becoming aware of communicating with other people in the group will be the single source of explanations for many different groups with different purposes as these are applied in different settings.

How can such an immensely wide range of experiences be explained while focusing on only one need? This is where a certain understanding of the systems approach may help, as will be explained in Chapters 1 and 2.

One explanation for all groups?

This question is taken up fully in Chapter 1. As already mentioned, the range of groupwork practices is very wide indeed. The present framework will not attempt to account for the whole range. I shall limit myself to exploring simpler groups. Many groups are time-limited; that is, the date of ending the group is known in advance. Such groups are not necessarily short-lived as some may contract to work for one or even two years. The deciding factor here is that a time-limit is chosen in advance. Such time-limited groups tend to show clearer patterns when compared to open-ended groups, where the duration of the group is not decided in advance. Therefore, only time-limited groups will be discussed in this book.

Even within time-limited groups, the range is still very wide. Again, for the sake of clarity, only some of these time-limited groups will be included. These groups will be the ones where the focus is on emphasising the interpersonal needs of group members. Interpersonal needs are usually related to roles which members assume; for example, the role of parents. Interpersonal needs can also be related to roles that members try to assume; for example, to be employed in a certain job the person has to accept the role of employee. At the same time interpersonal needs can also include roles that members have lost; for example the role of wife or husband when a spouse dies. Whatever these are, certain personal needs are associated with such social expectations. Combining social expectations with personal wishes leads people to realise their interpersonal roles. These roles will be the other focus of the present framework.

In contrast, very personal psychotherapeutic groups will not be included, nor will more social groups – aiming towards collective action. The framework will deal only with choices open to workers in time-limited groups that focus on interpersonal needs.

Another limitation will be accepted. This limitation concerns the difference between grouping people together and working with them as a group. It is possible to invite eight to ten people and let them do what they want. Some social clubs serve a very good purpose by grouping people in this way. Yet, the groupwork mentioned in this book will be different. Such groupwork always involves members and workers in becoming aware of what is going on in their group. Expecting members and workers to notice and reflect on their own relationship colours their group experiences in ways that are central to the present framework.

To summarise, *time-limited interpersonal groups that include increasing awareness of communication in the group will be the focus of the present framework.*

What choices are open to the worker?

More about this question appears in Chapter 1. In practice, the choice of how to work with each group is influenced by many aspects. At least five of these are almost obvious:

Group members' needs

The needs that bring people to groups should be paramount in choosing how to work with them. These needs may be more personal, such as the needs of the bereaved. The needs may be more interpersonal; for example, the needs of people who struggle with schizophrenia to master certain living skills. The needs may also be more social: black people who wish to assert their social identity, is an example.

Groupworkers' skills

It takes time and effort to master all the groupwork skills that are now available to practitioners. At each point in time some workers know more about creating an unstructured facilitative environment, while others are particularly adept at devising structured programmes. At the same time, some workers are more used to relying on activities for working with groups, while others are more at home when members sit around and are engaged only in discussion.

The agency

The resources the agency is able to provide influence the choice of approach too. If there is a clear structure for case-allowance, referral processes, supervision, and budget, more choices can be considered as compared to situations in which these resources are not available.

Legal context

The legal powers and responsibilities held by the agency often influence the groupwork approach practised. A clear example are the groups run in the criminal justice system where the obligations of probation workers to the court influence their approach to groupwork.

Messages from research

It goes without saying that practitioners have to be informed of research results about the likely outcomes of various groupwork approaches in helping different people. The problem is that, as yet, such research results are not easy to obtain.

If so many aspects influence the choice, should not each group be offered a totally different approach?

Is not each group totally different from any other?

Chapter 1 continues to deal with such questions. It has to be said that here is where answers begin to be a little more complicated. Ironically, the answer to this question is 'yes and no'.

Each group is likely to have some features unique to it. This is so because the above five aspects are likely to be combined differently for each group. So – yes, each group is likely to be different. Yet, no – in some respects, groups do show sufficient similarities so that we may compare and contrast one with all others; groups are also similar to one another. How can this be?

Eight to twelve people in a room with one or two workers may gather for very different reasons – personal, interpersonal, or social. Yet, once they gather in the room, these people cannot help getting involved in some ways. One way or another all groups begin to communicate. Even while members sit in silence they still influence one another, and therefore are already communicating. Thus, *finding what all groups have in common can be helped by focusing on the ways members and workers communicate.*

Becoming aware of this very universal experience of communicating leads to realising that another aspect is at work. As we become aware that we communicate, we encounter a paradox. This paradox surfaces whenever we begin to look for words that capture our experiences.

Groupworkers are also very likely to come across this paradox. Here is an example: in order to see how group members influence one another, we have to connect them to one another by focusing on the *interaction* between them, but to understand that interaction we need also to separate members as distinct *individuals*. A contradiction arises between focusing on separate individuals and focusing on connecting interactions. We resolve this contradiction when we understand that two levels of perception are involved.

Group interaction is one level of looking at communication. That interaction may be 'equally shared' or 'split', it may be 'symmetric' or 'complementary' and so on. A certain arrangement summarises members' interaction over and above the differences between them.

Looking at each member as an individual entails a different level. At this level the pattern adopted by each member; for example, that of placating, questioning, or encouraging, is discernible.

Groupwork involves the worker in continuously shuttling between these two levels of perception so that all members' needs are met.

We do need to separate each member from all others. Yet, at the same time, we also need to connect each member to all others so we can see the influences among them. Indeed, tension between separating and connecting seems inevitable and also confusing. How do we cope?

We do cope – by summarising. Individual differences and group interaction are, so to speak, put together in one bag. We then begin to talk about 'the group as a whole'. The group as a whole is constructed in many different ways, depending on practitioners' understanding of the processes involved. Consequently, groups have been described in terms such as 'dependent', 'productive', 'conflictual' and many more. The group as a whole is a third level, which we introduce in order to cope with the tension between the previous two. As Flemons (1991) showed, pursuing two opposite goals such as separating and connecting is possible when a third aspect is involved. The third aspect is often hidden or undeclared. Yet, the third aspect contains the apparent contradiction between the other two by explaining them. Indeed, we end up working in three simultaneous ways:

In one mode, we see each member as a *separate* individual.

In another mode, we observe the interaction that *connects* individuals.

In a third mode, we construct an image of the group as a whole that *completes* the picture by containing separate individuals and the interactions that connect them.

Graphically, the arrangement is as in Figure 1.

This triangular combination of *separating*, *connecting*, and *completing* seems to appear whenever we begin to choose words that encapsulate free-flowing experiences of communication. Therefore, this triangle is shared by all groups: all develop within the same 'three-cornered world'.

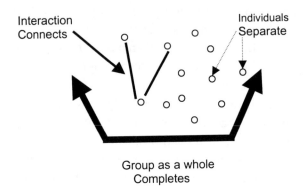

Figure 1 The three modes of perception

As will be explained in Chapter 1, Flemons' (1991) work suggests that this world stems from a certain paradox that I call *'the paradox of talk'*. Drawing on the work of Flemons (1991) it is possible to show that this paradox arises when we begin to look for words to convey what we experience. When we understand the paradox of talk we see that we have to separate perceptions from one another so that we can connect these to one another, and we have to connect perceptions to each other so we can separate these from one another. This 'strange loop' will be fully explained in Chapter 1. Here it is important to note that we cope with the apparent contradiction by discovering a third aspect which Flemons called 'completing'. The completing aspect contains the apparent contradictions and so – renders these meaningful.

Individuals, interaction, and the group as a whole are the elements of only one triangle that is parallel to the paradox of talk. Many other parallels to the paradox of talk will be explored in this book. All these parallels will show how a wide range of concepts can be linked to one and only one source: that initial paradox of talk. Paradoxes can be confusing but some are actually helpful. This particular paradox is so helpful because it lies behind all forms of groupwork, over and above the different goals and the various settings in which the groups are offered.

Indeed, when awareness of group dynamics is the focus, three other aspects always tend to surface: contents, process, and structure. Let me take up each separately.

Contents

People in the group talk about certain issues such as feeling they are different from everybody else, or dealing with doctors, or trying to find someone to help with shopping. These conversations often build up to themes such as trust, power, or mutual aid. Underlying these themes are often dilemmas. Trust can evoke the dilemma between the wish to belong and the need for autonomy; power can provoke the struggle between the desire to take charge of one's life and the craving for sound and reliable advice. These dilemmas surface in many different groups and, as will be explained, behind these dilemmas are value judgements held by the group members. Moral judgement operates by a set of codes that tell us what is 'bad' and should be eradicated, what is 'good' and should be pursued, and what is really inevitable and should be sustained. The latter helps us handle inevitable contradictions. In this sense, the contents can lead us to identifying the containing, or in Flemons' (1991) terms, 'Completing' aspect of the group experience.

Processes

There is a difference between what people say and the ways they say it. We usually refer to these differences as 'processes'. Sometimes the verbal and non-verbal messages are the same and at other times these are split in rather confusing ways. Processes of influence among people are even richer than that, and these occur in all groups, regardless of the differences among them. Processes flow continuously among people and in this sense, these experiences are parallel to the Connecting aspect of the paradox of talk.

Structure

Not only are moment-to-moment processes quite universal. When processes are repeated, these tend to give rise to patterns of behaviour and further on to positions of influence in each group. Some members become 'leaders' and others assume the roles of 'followers'. Some are 'jokers' and others are 'prophets of doom'. These positions may be temporary or may be long-standing. Either way, these roles build up to a structure. What is 'appropriate' to discuss and what is not, what is 'called for' and what is not – all are choices made in view of the structure of influence in the group. The workers are part of the structure, and they influence the contents as well as the processes too. Structural arrangements tend to introduce differences that separate people within the group and so – are parallel to the Separating aspect of the paradox of talk.

While groups differ a great deal they also show similarities in regard to contents, process, and structure. Together, contents, process, and structure will be called here 'the group's dynamics'.

Are the group's dynamics always the same?

This question takes up a great part of Chapter 2. I am afraid that the answer has to be, yet again: yes and no. Most groups begin and end in more or less the same ways. The dynamics of starting the group and of ending it appear remarkably similar in very different groups. So, there seems to be an obvious similarity. Yet, the middle periods of different groups vary considerably. The middle period of a group for adolescents in trouble with the law seems distinctly different from the middle period of a group for bereaved older adults.

Adolescents are often engaged in power issues at the interpersonal level, and this struggle gives rise to peer competition. Bereaved older adults often struggle with the impact of losing a spouse on far more personal and intimate areas in their lives. The experiences that these people consider most important relate to spontaneous identification and resonance with their peers, rather than competition for power.

How can a worker anticipate the middle period?

An answer is offered in Chapter 2, where the differences among prescribed, basic, and evolving designs of group stages are clarified. The reasons for preferring the evolving position towards group stages are outlined.

The middle period should meet the members' needs. That much is recognised by many. The problem is how to identify these needs specifically enough to know what to expect. This is a difficult problem, and the present framework can only begin to identify the questions that can help practitioners address it. Here it is assumed that all needs are expressed as various forms of communicating. In addition, a rather daring assumption is made. Imagine there was a general pool of groupwork experiences – experiences that are potentially relevant to all groups. Now consider how useful it would be if these stages could be rationally identified and explicitly explained in advance. If there was such an all-inclusive range, then it might be possible to identify the experiences that are most relevant to each group even before that group reaches the middle period.

Some groups would be expected to focus on interpersonal problem-solving; for example, in meeting the needs of adolescents to establish power positions among their peers. Such groups would be expected to focus on the stage called here 'the Empowerment phase' more than the free flowing intimate revelations that characterise the stage called 'the Mutuality phase'. Other groups would be expected to focus on revealing embarrassing and very personal experiences and even fantasies. Examples of such groups are those that aim to meet the needs of bereaved older adults who cope with the loss of a life-long partner. Therefore, such groups would be expected to focus on the stage called 'the Mutuality phase' more than the interpersonally competitive 'Empowerment phase'.

This is exactly what the present framework is designed to achieve. By analysing the communication needs of all groups, an inclusive blueprint of group stages will be suggested in Chapter 2. Describing such a sequence of experiences where contents, process, and structure coalesce in a particular way is not unusual. Many schemes of group development do just that when stages are described.

The difference between the present scheme and all others is in the detail. The present stance avoids prescribing all the stages for all groups and, at the same time, insists that all the stages are relevant to the field of groupwork as a whole. How can this double description make any sense?

The inclusive blueprint of group stages will be developed in Chapter 2 by focusing on another aspect of communication among people, called 'boundarying'.

What is involved in boundarying? You will have no doubt noticed that moments of totally open and spontaneous communication among people are rather rare, and therefore precious. Most of the time we select what we say to whom – we share some concerns with strangers, perhaps not more than the weather. Yet, we share our deeper anxieties and also joys with our loved ones.

In between are hosts of people in different proximity to us – colleagues, bosses, friends and acquaintances. We choose how much to disclose to each according to the position each occupies in our lives. We also change such positions; for example, when a person who has been an acquaintance becomes a friend. The same process of selection is likely to happen in groups too. Group members boundary their relationships with other members and with the worker. Most people tend to begin by putting up the barriers that allow them to focus on social concerns first. More personal issues are opened up later – when these are relevant to the purpose of the group, and particularly when members are convinced that it is safe enough to do so.

Such changes of opening and closing boundaries regulate the distance among members and between them and the outside world. Group development will be assumed to evolve while group members open their boundaries to some issues and close these boundaries to others. This opening and closing of boundaries will be called simply 'boundarying'; a term borrowed from James Durkin (1981).

How does this inclusive blueprint help?

Understanding the inclusive blueprint of group stages will lead to seeing the possible foci of the middle period. The middle period may focus on dealing with authority figures, or handling peer competition, or removing certain taboos; or it may include a very unstructured period of spontaneous resonance among members, or even mourning the loss of the group. The middle period may also be a combination of some of these themes, and in some groups it may actually include all of these concerns. In this sense, the middle period of each group may be different. Yet, the difference is not likely to disconnect one group from all others. The difference is more likely to show that each group emphasises some experiences more than others. This is so because the experiences described above will not be chosen arbitrarily. These experiences will be derived from the same pool of potential stages of group development. Here are typical stages:

- The struggle with authority figures tends to arise during the *Authority* crisis.

- Peer competition is often handled during the *Empowerment* phase.

- Secrets are likely to be revealed during the *Intimacy* crisis.

- Spontaneous resonance among members is likely to arise during the *Mutuality* phase.

- Mourning the end of the group can be expected during the *Separation* crisis.

You will notice that some stages are called *'phases'* while others are described as *'crises'*. The difference between the two was first identified by Levine (1979), but it will be explained from a systems point of view in Chapter 2. Some groups will be expected to develop only through some of the phases and others will be expected to experience all the five phases of the blueprint. At the same time, certain groups will be likely to go through certain crises but others may well not feel the need for any of these at all. Many other combinations of phases and crises are certainly to be expected.

Therefore, while each group may choose certain stages as its focus, all groups will be related to one another. This dual character will be secured since the different range of experiences in each group will be seen as merely a different combination of the same aspects. These same aspects will form a three-cornered world; that is, will be parallel to the aspects that define the paradox of talk. As all aspects will be parallel to the same paradox, all the experiences will be merely different combinations of the same elements.

You may know about such a possibility from painting. You probably know that the rainbow comprises only three colours: red, yellow, and blue. All other colours are combinations of these basic three. The same will apply to any practice with each group. Each groupwork approach will be simply a different mix of the same three aspects. In this sense, each group will be different from and at the same time also similar to all others.

I shall call this way of identifying how each group may develop the 'evolving view of group development'. The evolving view gives each practitioner the freedom to find the approach that suits each group best, and at the same time, this view enables each practitioner to compare and contrast the chosen approach to all others. This combination of freedom to choose and the responsibility to relate, is part of the inclusive position that lies behind the present framework, and is where Part 1 will end.

Once I know what to expect – how do I know what to do?

Applications of the inclusive blueprint are the subject of Part 2. The proposed framework will not tell you everything you want to know about what to do. As mentioned at the beginning, the present modest scope stems from the very wide range of aspects that influence groupworkers when they choose what to do. Here it will be possible to suggest only how each worker may be helped by understanding the group's dynamics.

Workers can become involved in everything that happens in the group. Workers who do this find themselves rather overwhelmed and easily confused because so much tends to happen in each group. Most workers identify some priorities. These priorities direct the worker in deciding what calls for her involvement. The four chapters of Part 2 will demonstrate how priorities may be determined. These chapters are constructed as pairs, and each pair includes two stages. This will be the order of chapters:

Chapter 3: Forming the Group and the Engagement Phase.
Chapter 4: Authority Crisis and the Empowerment Phase.
Chapter 5: Intimacy Crisis and the Mutuality Phase.

Chapter 6: Separation Crisis and the Termination Phase.

Yet, all the chapters will refer to one example of direct work with one group. The group chosen is one for parents who have run into difficulties raising their children. Each stage will begin with a brief verbatim example. The example will be a condensed version of exchanges that characterise that particular stage. Discussion will then follow to explain how workers may choose to be involved in the three aspects of the group's dynamics: contents, levels, and process. Separate comments about each may clarify their relevance.

What calls for involvement: The contents

Experienced workers convey their involvement more often towards those themes in which quite a number of members seem to be involved. Exchanges in the group may take many directions, but sooner or later members tend to return to the same concern: trust, power, secrets or any other. These shared concerns are often seen as priorities for the worker's involvement. Within the present framework, the worker will be particularly sensitive to moments when members struggle with apparent opposites: to trust or retain autonomy, to lead or to be led, and many others. Such apparent opposites often indicate dilemmas, and dilemmas are often openings for discovering new solutions. This is why the worker does need to listen carefully to the contents of members' conversations. The present framework will identify some of the major dilemmas that are likely to arise during each of the stages of group development.

When to become involved: The levels

Having identified that certain experiences do call for their involvement, many workers also ask themselves whether the group is ready to take up the emerging issue at that particular juncture. Usually two considerations are on workers' minds when they grapple with this question. One is whether the emerging issue is relevant to this particular group. For example, in a group that prepares foster parents who had met already for three weeks, a number of members may refer to the subject of traffic jams in the city. Although the worker can see that ultimately everything is connected, at this stage of the group's development the worker may consider traffic jams to be a topic of low priority. Therefore, the worker may intervene to delay such a discussion to informal conversations outside the group.

However, if during the second session of that group, quite a number of members come back to the issue of helping a fostered child explore their growing sexuality, the worker may form a different judgement. The worker may well judge the topic to be highly relevant to this group. The relevance will not be in question, but timing may well be.

For various reasons, groups may jump into the deep end of personal explorations very early on. Experienced workers usually appreciate that such a rapid movement towards such an intense level of intimacy may not be helpful to most group members. Usually a period in which less personal and more interpersonal issues are explored is needed first. During such a period the parents' sense of competence is established and their confidence grows that other members respect their own ways of responsibly raising their children. Often it is only on this basis that parents can freely and openly explore the depth of childrens' sexuality and particularly their own personal feelings while discussing sexuality with the children they will foster.

How does the worker sense premature disclosures? Here is where identifying that part of the structure which will be called 'level' seems to help. Whether explicitly or implicitly, each group seems to develop a certain understanding about the agreed relevance of various topics. Some topics are social in that these concern all people regardless of the differences between them. Gender differences are a good example of social issues because everybody, regardless of other differences, is either male or female. Other topics are clearly personal: these concern the ways each individual is different from others. Particular religious beliefs may be highly personal for some people, and sexual orientation is often considered rather personal. In our society, certain weaknesses; for example, the inability to read, also belong to this category.

In between the social and the personal is the interpersonal level. People often say: 'As a woman I feel that ...', or 'As a Muslim, for me it is ...'. When they say so, these people begin with identifying a social role: that of a woman, or that of a Muslim. Yet, they do not stop at the social level. These people then add their own interpretation of the meaning of that role to them. As pointed out before, when a person creates a personal version of a social role, that person is referring to the interpersonal level.

Groupworkers can choose when to become involved by identifying the level at which each group can work well at each point in time. The present framework will identify the likely level: whether social, or interpersonal, or personal, for each stage of group development over time.

Having realised that members are involved in a relevant dilemma and that the level of exchanges is such that group members can grapple with it constructively, the worker still faces another question. The question now is how to become involved.

How to become involved: The skills

Experienced workers try to follow the flow of processes. This they do by resorting to certain skills. From a systems point of view, all those things that a worker may do can be divided into three types.

The worker can initiate responses when he or she senses that something is missing; for example, members avoid concrete details when describing certain difficulties. Workers may also initiate the lessening of messages that group members use excessively; for example, when accusations keep flying around the room. In this book both types of the skills involved will be called *'stabilising'*. When resorting to stabilising skills the worker is steering the group process towards a desirable range of exchanges. In the first example, the worker steers the group towards offering concrete descriptions more often. In the second, the worker steers that group towards resorting to accusations less frequently. In both, the worker's involvement contributes towards stabilising the group process towards a certain range of experiences.

On the other hand, the worker can also respond to unexpected expressions in the group – particularly those that stand out as different and even 'un-called for'. Rather than dampening such 'disturbances', the worker can respond in ways that intensify the deviation. Intensifying disturbing experiences can help the group open up areas of exploration that have been avoided up to that point. Such modes of responding will be called here *'amplifying'*.

Whether stabilising or amplifying, the worker always has to help group members make sense of their experiences. There are many ways of facilitating such understanding. The worker can raise questions about the meaning of exchanges. The worker can also comment on the dynamics of the exchanges. At times the worker may even offer an interpretation of aspects that seem to stir up members without them noticing that these aspects confuse their involvement with others. The range of skills that help members make sense of their experiences will be called here *'clarifying'*.

The accounts of direct practice will include incidents of resorting to all three types of skills: stabilising, amplifying, and clarifying. Some examples of the specific skills that come within each of these three categories will be mentioned. Above all, how to combine such different skills during each stage of the group's development will be the main focus.

Stabilising, amplifying, and clarifying may well be the lion's share of the worker's involvement. In addition, there are moments when the worker should not do any of the above. It is important to know when to take a back seat and let members sort out the dilemmas that trouble them by themselves. Some practitioners call this ability to be a supportive witness of others' struggles, 'containing'. Indeed, one of the benefits of the inclusive framework is in identifying these moments, when all the worker has to do is to enable members to sustain inevitable and enabling tensions between polarities of certain dilemmas. Throughout Part 2, this need to sustain polarities will be identified for each stage too.

By now, you may be just a little apprehensive. The next question on your mind may well be this:

What will be the end result?

Continuous growth and development has been the hallmark of the systems approach as it has been applied to more and more areas of practice. For now, the journey will result in a conceptual framework that enables practitioners to resort to an evolving view of group stages.

In the most immediate sense, this inclusive stance will offer practitioners *tools* with which they shall be able to focus their involvement in the various aspects of group dynamics and a *language* that will enable them to explain what they do.

In a more general sense, the evolving view will give practitioners the freedom to identify their practice as separate from that of all others. At the same time, practitioners will be able also to connect what they do with many different forms of groupwork practice.

This dual purpose will be contained within the inclusive stance adopted throughout this book, and the final chapter, on wider implications, will explore this point. The inclusive stance avoids the extreme of pragmatism that leads to fragmentation. This stance also avoids the extreme of integration that can lead to stagnation. Instead, the inclusive stance lays the foundations for continuous exploration and innovation. This invitation to 'pick and mix' gives each practitioner the freedom to choose their own approach with the responsibility to relate their choice to the approaches chosen by others.

The ideas are organised in a rather straightforward fashion. Perhaps it may help to summarise the topics in the order in which these will appear.

Summary: How this book is organised

Three parts comprise this book. First comes this Introduction which sets out the scene and identifies the major issues to be raised.

Then comes Part 1, 'Evolving a Framework', where the problem of choosing a groupwork approach is reviewed, and the concepts necessary to understand the inclusive stance are explained. This part consists of two chapters:

Chapter 1, 'Connecting the Fragments: The role of paradox' begins with the problem. The wide variety of practices has led to groupwork being badly fragmented. As a result, it is very difficult to compare and contrast practices, let alone work towards improvements. To begin tackling this problem groupwork is first defined. The range of groupwork practices is narrowed to time-limited groups that focus on interpersonal issues, and the range of issues explored is limited to the basic dynamics of each group. The advantages of the systems approach for exploring the relevant issues are then highlighted. A particular strand of the systems approach is followed here, where communication and the paradox it involves are central. The advantages of this strand of the systems approach may not be immediately obvious. Therefore, it is stressed that these advantages are realised when we learn to draw parallels to the structure of the central paradox. Then groupwork is described as evolving within a parallel 'three-cornered world': contents, structure and process.

Chapter 2, 'Stages in a Three-Cornered World', applies the ideas in Chapter 1. The basic dynamics of all groups are explored as a communication cycle. That cycle is comprised of eight stages that can be derived from seeing groupwork as evolving within a three-cornered world. First, the various approaches to identifying group stages are reviewed. Then the four converging features are identified. A systems view of group development is offered to explain why these converging features may be universal. Drawing parallels to the central paradox, a three-cornered world is constructed. Within this triangle, the ability to open and close boundaries is shown to be vital in explaining the order in which group stages seem to emerge. Understanding such acts of 'boundarying' leads to constructing the communication cycle of all potential group stages. This cycle is then shown to fluctuate between phases and crises. When the contents of group stages are added the ground is ready for seeing the potential range of stages that may arise in all groups: the inclusive blueprint of group stages. The chapter ends with a comment on the need to adopt 'a binocular view' so that certain stages are chosen for each group while keeping in mind the whole range of the inclusive blueprint.

In Part 2, 'Applying the Inclusive Blueprint', the concepts of the proposed three-cornered world are applied to a practice example. This example is of working with one group through all the eight stages of the inclusive blueprint. After demonstrating each stage, comments are made about the relevance of this stage to various groups, the contents involved, the level at which this stage tends to evolve, and the processes of change that may be mobilised.

A brief section about Wider Implications rounds off the discussion with further reflections on the powers of paradox. The powers of paradox are shown to be known even to children. For the adult practitioner the powers of paradox are helpful in articulating groupwork stages, in promoting genuine accountability, in enhancing a dynamic sense of competence, in increasing flexibility, and in ensuring inclusiveness.

Overall, it is probably true that specific terms and particular concepts are needed for a systems understanding of complex experiences that arise in groups. Yet, examples of each of the terms will be offered. Some readers may want to read the detailed practice examples of working with the same group during all the eight stages of the inclusive blueprint first. It may then be easier to see how the terms and concepts explain practice.

A final note of caution

As I let this book into the public domain, I can hear voices protesting: what about the full depth of genuine relationships? What about the full political context? Are the concepts fully and totally articulated? Can all these ideas be researched empirically?

Indeed, each of these questions is entirely valid. All I can do by way of response is to lean on Martin Buber (1963) who wrote somewhat ironically:

> It is not nice...to first hook me on the pathos of 'all or nothing' and then prove the impossibility of my so-called claim. I do not know what 'all' is nor what is 'nothing', both seem to me the fruit of imagination, and what I mean concerns a degree of possibility. (Buber, 1963, p.148).

I hope you will be able to settle for Buber's 'degree of possibility' and find your own way to filling the gaps and modifying ideas. Who knows, future dialogue may yield some further choices that can only enhance groupwork practice further.

Part 1

Evolving a Framework

This first part lays the foundations for the ones to come. The purpose of this book is discussed, major concepts are proposed, and an underlying rationale for choosing group stages is clarified. These basic issues are explored in two chapters.

Chapter 1: Connecting the Fragments: the Role of Paradox, clarifies the problem of fragmentation in groupwork practice. Communication is suggested as the thread that connects all forms of practice and can help us resolve that problem. When communication is chosen as the focus, a paradox emerges at its heart. Like all paradoxes, this 'paradox of talk' is a particular triangle. Drawing parallels to that paradox enables us to see many practice situations as 'three-cornered worlds', so we may be able to compare and contrast these to one another more easily.

Chapter 2: Stages in a Three-cornered World, capitalises on the concepts suggested in Chapter 1. In Chapter 2 these concepts are expanded to suggest a rationale of the stages of group development, and a common pool of eight stages from which very different forms of groupwork practice may be derived.

CHAPTER ONE

Connecting the Fragments

The Role of Paradox

Here is a brief summary of this chapter.

Seen as a whole, groupwork practice is fragmented to such extent that it is very difficult to compare and contrast various forms of practice let alone improve it. This degree of fragmentation is the main problem.

After presenting the problem, groupwork is defined as time-limited and focused on interpersonal needs of group members. Rather than elaborating on the various methods employed in different versions of groupwork, this framework deals with the basic dynamics of groups. These dynamics are manifest in various combinations of the contents, structure, and process that arise in each group.

The basic dynamics are examined from a systems point of view. Within this view the thread connecting all groups is communication. The focus on communication connects all groups to one another because some form of communication takes place in all groups. While communicating we usually need words. When we begin to look for the words that may capture our experiences we realise that we are involved in a paradox, which I shall call 'the paradox of talk'. Three aspects mutually define one another to form this paradox: separating, connecting, and completing. This triangle of concepts can be helpful when we develop the ability to draw parallels to it at various levels of communication. One of these parallels concerns the ways contents, structure and process influence one another. These influences are central to groupwork because together they capture a great deal of group dynamics. Furthermore, contents, structure and process – the three aspects of group dynamics, can be seen as three corners of a world that parallels the triangle involved in the paradox of talk.

Due to the self-containing nature of this paradox, each of the major aspects of group dynamics is itself another 'three-cornered world': a mini-universe revolving around the same paradox of talk. Each of these mini three-cornered worlds defines one of the major aspects: contents, structure and process. Together these three aspects can be used to map out the stages of group development. The discussion will follow these headings:

> The problem of fragmentation
>
> Groupwork: time-limited and interpersonal
>
> Basic dynamics
>
> Advantages of the systems approach
>
> Systems, communication and the paradox of talk
>
> Drawing parallels
>
> Groupwork in a three-cornered world: process, structure (levels) and contents

First, let me introduce the problem.

Helping the bereaved

Educating parents

Training young women to assert themselves

Supporting carers of long term patients

Stopping adolescents from committing crimes

The list above is only a small sample of goals pursued through groupwork. In social work alone, Doel and Sawdon (1999b) have identified 25 different groups offered by one social work agency.

How do workers pursue each of these goals? Intuition alone would suggest that helping the bereaved is rather different from teaching young women to assert themselves, and that supporting carers is quite different from crime prevention.

The problem of fragmentation

How do workers choose the approach for each of these very different groups? Do they choose the approach that interests them most? Do they do what their managers tell them to do? Do they practice whatever approach they were taught on a previous course? If workers mix different groupwork approaches, how do they choose the particular combination? As long as groupwork practice is so fragmented, it will remain virtually impossible to answer such questions. Indeed, when Vasco and Dryden (1994) tried to answer these questions in regard to psychotherapists, they found that the choices were influenced more by practitioners' personal beliefs and their own clinical experience than by research outcomes and rational considerations. Yet, we cannot avoid another question. Do groupworkers achieve their aims? Can we show the outcomes expected of us? Outcome studies, of groupwork on its own, are not so widely available. The most comprehensive data available combine groupwork and group psychotherapy together. These were reviewed by Bednar and Kaul (1994) who analysed many studies of experiential groups, and were able to point out considerable achievements. Yet, even these rigorous commentators point out that 'it is empirically and intuitively obvious that not all groups have had uniformly beneficial results' (Bednar and Kaul 1994, p.632).

Of course, Bednar and Kaul (1994) were able to comment only on those groups that had been subjected to research. As every practitioner knows, many groups are not researched. If we considered these groups too, we would probably have to be somewhat worried about the number of groups that had not had beneficial results.

Indeed, some empirical studies have been conducted in this area: for example, Kivlighan and Goldfire (1991), Kivlighan and Quigley (1991), Kivlighan, Multon, and Brossart (1996), and Ponze (1991). Each of these authors has studied group-related aspects, and valuable insights have arisen out of these authors' works, but these findings are still isolated from one another. Each study naturally focuses on an existing area of practice. Since each of these areas is different, it is difficult to compare various aspects of these findings to one another, as each may include idiosyncratic aspects emphasised by each practitioner.

How can we show beneficial results more often? Bednar and Kaul (1994, p.634) suggest that the reports available to them 'include few conceptual variables that are indigenous to group treatment'. They strongly advocate the painstaking work of relating specifically group processes to the desired outcomes. They further urge us to increase the conceptual clarity of our practice so that different outcomes can be compared to one another and replicated: clearer and more precise definitions of each aspect of working with each group are needed.

We need one set of concepts that connects very different practices. Such a framework has to be developed by logic; that is, by deductively deriving ideas in ways that preserve the connections among them. So, the challenge remains: how to integrate various findings within a framework that may serve as a unifying guide to working with many different groups.

Before the constructing of such a framework can begin, the area of groupwork has to be defined a little more narrowly.

Groupwork: Time-limited and interpersonal

Groups have been used to pursue many different human needs for a long time, and major applications are reviewed in the special issues of the journal *Groupwork* (Issues 11.3, 1999 and 12.1, 2000). Personal growth, occupational therapy, mental health, social work, community development, social action, health promotion, palliative care, criminal justice and community centred learning are all represented. Of course, no single book can capture all this variety, let alone shed light on practice with all of them.

The range will have to be narrowed for useful concepts to be clarified within one book. Here I shall be focusing only on certain types of groupwork: those which *include a time limit while focusing on interpersonal concerns.*

Including a time-limit

Some groups are set up to continue for as long as group members feel the group is helping them: these are open-ended groups. Other groups begin with an agreement to end the group at a certain point in time. Such a time limit seems to vary considerably: six months, a year, or even two years may be contracted. It is not clear yet what difference the length of time makes. However, practitioners' accounts suggest that agreeing on a time limit in advance may focus group members' minds on achieving certain goals before the end of the group. Perhaps this is the reason for the apparent clearer sense of direction group members show in time-limited groups compared to that of open-ended ones. Merely because their pattern appears more clearly, time-limited groups will be the focus of this framework.

Interpersonal focus

In some groups people come together to explore how to change their environment. Social action, where members focus mainly on obtaining resources; for example, a club, which they may use in new and liberating ways, is a clear example. A clear example of this direction is the work of Mullender and Ward (1991). In other groups, members focus on their internal experiences – such as how being depressed may be related to harbouring repressed memories of being rejected in the past. Such groups are usually called 'group psychotherapy' (for examples, see Aveline and Dryden 1988; Bernard and MacKenzie 1994).

The groups discussed here fall in-between these two end points. People are involved in many different relationships – some very personal and intimate, such as those between lovers, and others clearly social; such as the relationships among members of a political party. In between are relationships that can be framed around the *interpersonal roles* people occupy.

Some people may want help while coping with a certain role in which they find themselves unexpectedly; for example, that of being bereaved. Others may want to let go of roles they have entered in the past; for example, the role of offender. Yet a third group may wish to acquire new roles; for example, that of being women who are assertive. All will be paying attention to certain roles. A large part of social group work (Brown 1992) and many approaches to group counselling (Brammer, Abrego and Shostrom 1993; Tudor 1999) deal with such needs.

When interpersonal roles are considered two aspects emerge: one refers to socially prescribed expectations. Something is already known about ways and means of pursuing interpersonal goals that are related to being in these roles. For example, in most cultures, certain behaviours are expected of people who are parents (setting a moral example, providing for the physical needs of their children etc.). These behaviours are known in advance in each culture and are often passed on from generation to generation.

Yet, some of the behaviours associated with these roles touch upon very personal areas in the lives of those concerned. In industrial societies, intimate relationships between parents and children are also expected. To develop some degree of intimacy each person has to find some individual ways of expressing care, concern, and affection. These ways cannot be directly taught but have to be found by each parent afresh. Therefore, each person has also to find personal ways of coping with the socially prescribed role; be it that of a parent, or an adolescent, or a woman. In short, social roles have to be individually personalised. This is why such roles also have an emergent aspect in addition to the prescribed one. In groupwork people come together to explore how to cope with existing roles, how to shed previous ones, and how to develop new roles. Yet all these roles include a clear interpersonal focus – some aspects are known about these roles and can be directly learned, while other aspects have to emerge for each individual through the personal exchanges among group members. Metaphorically speaking, interpersonal roles are hand-written: while the letters, like social expectations, may all be the same, each person develops a personal style of handwriting, the script of interpersonal roles that suits that person best.

This interpersonal focus leads to another feature of groupwork. In order to cope better with certain roles, or to shed some, or to learn new ones – change is necessary. In groupwork such changes are pursued through enabling members to become more *aware* of their relationships: inside the group and also outside it. If so, then it is probably possible to define groupwork just a little more specifically.

Groupwork takes place when:

> *A small number of people* usually between 6 and 12,

> who all have *equal formal status* of members,

> are involved with one or two groupworkers in *face to face* interaction while considering themselves to be a group, which will:

> meet *regularly* for a period of time set *in advance*,

> become more *aware* of their relationships,

> focus on their *interpersonal* roles inside the group as well as outside it, and take an active part in *changing* these roles.

With this definition in hand it may be possible to move forward now. Yet, even within this time-limited interpersonal focus, too many issues may arise: the setting of practice, the particular techniques, the legal constraints – none of these will be explored here. Instead, I shall distil all these concerns down to one essential phenomenon: the basic dynamics of each group.

Basic dynamics

Up to now I have narrowed down the present subject to time-limited interpersonal groups. Yet, even this area is too vast. Studying groups, even when so limited, may involve many different levels: the group composition, members' networks (family, employment, religious affiliation, cultural pursuits, friendships), the agency within which the group is offered, the workers' training and supervision, and specific skills these workers apply; all these levels influence the outcomes of groupwork, but none will be included here. The reason is totally practical: space does not allow discussion of these very important aspects.

Instead, the focus will be on one area – that of changing role relationships: among group members, between them and the groupworkers, and in group members' immediate environment. In so doing, I shall accept the advice given by Yalom (1995) to group psychotherapists:

> When therapists form a new therapy group in some specialized setting or for some specialized population, the first step…is to determine the appropriate goal and then the therapeutic factors most likely to be helpful for that particular group. All else, all matters of therapeutic technique, follow from that framework. (Yalom 1995, pp.100–101)

In groupwork it is more appropriate to talk about facilitative rather than therapeutic conditions. Yet, the same logic applies. Relationships in the group will be seen as the facilitative factors that have to be engendered when members make changes in interpersonal relationships. Of course there are many ways of pursuing change – through a well-constructed programme, through activities, through homework assignments, or through spontaneous interaction within the group. The choice of method will be left to each practitioner. The assumption is that a groupworker who understands the basic dynamics is likely to find the technique that facilitates the dynamics best in pursuing certain goals, with people of identifiable abilities, within a specific setting, and within a particular legal framework. As long as the basic dynamics of the group are such that members can use the chosen method for learning, quite a number of methods may well be suitable. The choice of method is expected to emerge out of understanding the group's dynamics.

In this book, the understanding of each group's basic dynamics will be enhanced through the systems approach.

Advantages of the systems approach

What theory will let groupworkers compare and contrast their practice with so many others? Because of the interpersonal focus, a highly versatile theory is needed. This theory will have to help to account for at least three main issues. First, the theory will have to connect members' experiences inside the group to their life in the world outside it. Second, that theory will have to explain many ways in which members change their roles. Third, the theory will have to be one that elucidates the ways people in very different roles make sense of their relationships.

Indeed – such theory already exists as 'general systems theory', and the work of Wilden (1980) is probably one of the most generically thorough explorations of it. In group psychotherapy, the volume edited by James Durkin (1981) is of equal importance. In a small way, I attempted to suggest how various types of group psychotherapy could be compared to one another in terms of the feedback processes prevalent in each (Manor 1994). Yet, because there are by now so many different meanings to this term, I prefer to refer to 'the systems approach'. Specific applications exist too. In group psychotherapy, the work of Agazarian (1997) is a prime example of applying highly evolved concepts from the systems approach to psychotherapeutic practice. Agazarian's concept of 'boundary modification' is very relevant to the practice discussed here. Likewise, the work of McClure (1998), who drew on chaos theory, illuminates very well the experiences of open-ended personal growth groups, where people join together with the all-embracing goal of expanding their potential. Although independently developed, quite a number of the concepts applied by McClure will also appear in the present framework, but these will be given different and simpler names.

In groupwork, the systems approach has been used already by some authors. However, up to now the application of the systems approach to groupwork has been partial. Doel and Sawdon (1999a) resorted to the systems approach as an overall umbrella, without the details which distinguish it from other theories. Donigian and Malnati (1997) concentrated on the structural aspects of the systems approach in their 'triadic model' without articulating change processes and how meaning is generated. Transformational change, which is so central to systems thinking (Manor 1997), cannot be explained within their model.

The present framework will capitalise on all the aspects of the systems approach by following a particular path. The systems approach will be seen focusing on communication among people, and particularly on becoming aware that we are communicating. When we become aware of communicating in words we experience a paradox. As will be explained, paradoxes always involve three aspects, therefore – it is necessary to 'think in threes'; to see every issue as three-dimensional. Indeed, the present framework is of a 'three-cornered world' that revolves around a paradox. Within this paradoxical framework it will be possible to:

- Separate as well as connect parts and whole (for example individual members and group interaction). This will help the understanding of what is meant by 'group stage'.

- Clarify boundary issues inside the group as well as between the group and the outside world. This will enable to identify the 'level' at which the group is engaged, and external influences on group members.

- Identify different change processes – particularly linear and transformational change. This difference will explain the dynamics of stages as being either that of a 'phase' or that of a 'crisis'.

- Elucidate themes as reflecting dilemmas with which group members struggle during their work together. These dilemmas lie behind group members' explicit, or overt, involvement in certain issues that the groupworker has to understand.

Here are the main features of the present understanding of the systems approach.

Systems, communication and the paradox of talk

'We cannot not communicate' is probably the most famous slogan of the systems approach. Why do we still think that this is true? Influences among group members flow in many directions at once – that is why working with a group is such an intricate endeavour. Yet, members do not necessarily sit in the group with the intention of communicating with one another. Sometimes members really want to communicate and at other times they do not. Still, even when nobody wants to communicate, influences reverberate in the room. Even when everybody sits in silence, communication is going on. How is this possible? We sit in silence – nobody is saying a word, yet we are surrounded by beings who are, at least physically, similar to us. So, we assume that we know what each of these beings is experiencing – the same as us, the opposite of what we feel, or a combination of these experiences. Whatever our guess, we are influenced by the experience. Therefore, communication is going on. The reason is probably the undeclared and sometimes unrecognised identification among people.

Because we cannot not communicate; that is, communication is inevitable, it seems a good common ground for many different explanations. As groups continue to communicate all the time, communication can be the connecting thread among very different groups. Yet, in groupwork we do not merely communicate – we deliberately enhance awareness of communication. This focus on awareness is the second layer of the connecting thread. To see this, it is worth taking a close look at the very process of becoming aware that we communicate. What happens when we begin to become aware that we communicate? This question has intrigued many, and the work of Bateson (1971, 1979) has inspired many applications to practice, particularly in family therapy. At a more general level, I have found Flemons' (1991) analysis particularly informative in this respect.

For this reason Flemons' (1991) work will underpin the present systems view, but I shall simplify his remarkable contribution, limiting my discussion to the aspects needed to construct the connecting thread. To explain the present view, I have to outline some basic processes. Let me begin with an example:

Here you are – at the beginning of the first session with a new group. You look around; everybody else is sitting there looking at you. You realise, 'Well, they've all turned up – I've got a group to work with.'

How did you arrive at this realisation? To begin with, you were looking for words that will account for what is going on. The words you chose focused on the question of whether people have turned up. You could have focused on a different question: are the chairs comfortable, or is the lighting pleasant? Your intentional act, of looking for a group, led you to saying that a potential group was present. A real event was taking place: people were entering the room. In addition, you 'constructed' that event to mean that a potential group was present in that room. Your perception was a combination of an external reality and an internal verbal construction of it (Speed 1991).

Next you realise that all the members have turned up: nobody is missing. How do you know that? You know it since you have met these people before, at least as a list of names on paper. You have already marked them as different from other people who appear on other lists. In short, you have already made a distinction between two types of people: those who are expected in this group, and those who are not.

Knowing always involves making a distinction between one thing and another.

When we resort to words we choose to mark out something – bring it to the fore. We distinguish this 'thing' from the rest, which we relegate to the background. We separate out something in order to know it: you have separated out the people who belong to the group in order to know them. Therein lies a paradox.

Separating and connecting

In order to separate out one thing from the other we need also to connect it to the other. Why is this so?

In the present example, you were able to know that the people in the room were separate from others since you had already identified others as *not* belonging to the group. When you excluded those others, you resorted to a yardstick; a criterion that showed that they were different. Yet, by excluding the others you *referred* to the people that you did invite. You were able to say who you did *not* invite by saying which people you *did* invite. You were comparing the uninvited people to the invited members. You were not just separating, you were also connecting the two by separating them.

In order to know one thing it is necessary to *separate* it from the other which is possible only by also *connecting* that thing to the other.

Everything you distinguish from another can be recognised only by referring to that other. Every negation also involves affirmation. Every 'no' also involves 'yes'. This paradoxical nature of talking is not unique to groupwork. We are involved in the paradox every day. Here is an example:

Perhaps you remember waking up early in the morning. You are a bit dazed and words are just not available yet. Eventually you do ask yourself: is it already daytime or is it still night? You are unsure. Indeed, the difference seems surprisingly elusive. It is then that you probably realise that it is brighter than you expected, yet too dark to get up. Later on, when you have fully recovered the use of words you may reflect on the fact that the difference between day and night is relative: every hour is relatively closer to daytime or relatively closer to night-time – nothing is really absolute. So – how do you decide that it is daytime? You know it, since you judge it not to be night-time. How do you know it is not night-time? Well, you know this since there is enough light to indicate to you that it can be called daytime.

Why is the difference between day and night so elusive? The answer is simple: because the earth revolves around the sun, the earth is continuously subjected to changes between light and darkness, and thus day and night mutually define one another; you have to refer to one in order to identify the other. The movement of the earth around the sun introduces a third dimension to the duality of day and night. This third dimension completes the picture by explaining it.

Completing

The third dimension, just mentioned, is needed in order to make sense of what we see. In the initial example, you were, so to speak, looking with two eyes: one could see each member, Jack, Jill, Harry and more; the other eye was watching how they related to one another – their interaction. Of course you were not simply spying on members to detect how they interacted. You were keeping an eye on the interaction to see what you could do to enable members to become 'a group'. In other words, you were already constructing an overall view of the group as a whole. This ability to form a complete picture of the parts is vital.

The complete picture of the group is different from the sum of the attributes of its members (the parts). Certain phenomena can be seen only when these people form a group and not while they remain isolated individuals: pressure for conformity, mutual support, competing for your attention – all these are group-as-a-whole phenomena. Forming a view of the group as a whole is an example of emphasising the *completing* mode of communication.

Together, separating, connecting, and completing are the three corners of the paradox that emerge when awareness of communication is expressed in words. Figure 1.1 is an example of this triangle. The chart refers to a situation where a minority of three members dominates the majority of five. You will realise that it is necessary to separate the three members on the right from the rest in order to see them as a dominating sub-group. You also have to connect that dominant minority to the rest in order to see a submissive majority. The construct of the group-as-a-whole, of 'a dependent group', completes the picture; helping you to see how both sides are trapped in a disabling arrangement that keeps them dependent on the workers who have to mediate the tensions between the two.

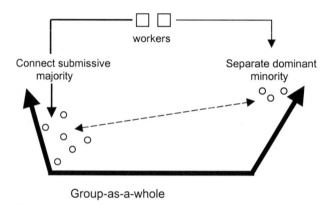

Figure 1.1 Completing a view of the group by Separating and Connecting its members

As Figure 1.1 shows, to fluctuate between separating and connecting we need to *complete* the picture; rendering it a meaningful whole.

> *I shall call this constellation of separating, connecting, and completing 'the paradox of talk' because this paradox arises when we look for words to capture our experiences.*

THE THREE-CORNERED WORLD AS A HOLOGRAM

Seeing all groupwork as grounded in the paradox of talk may be likened to creating a hologram. The hologram is one plate of metal upon which many images are imprinted. Depending on the angle of holding this plate, different images appear. The same approach will be taken here. As you will see now, the paradox of talk already contains the elements that make up all the concepts, which will follow. This holographic nature of the framework is helpful in pursuing a major goal: it ensures that concepts are related to one another. In this sense, the present framework is rather similar to the 'creative paradigm' developed by Peile (1994). You will see that the concepts developed now will be constructed as triangles that parallel the paradox of talk.

Drawing parallels is vital for the inclusive stance. Therefore, before the paradox of talk is applied, the skill of drawing parallels has to be described.

Drawing parallels

The arms and the legs are not the same – this is obvious enough. Yet, these limbs are not totally different either. What is the similarity between the legs and the arms? Well, they do come in pairs, each pair protrudes out of the torso, and each limb is divided into three sections. So, although the arms and the legs are used for different purposes and stretch out of the body at different points, their structures mirror one another. We say that the arms and the legs are parallel.

In general systems theory, some structures are recognised as having the same form; these structures are said to be 'isomorphic'. When two structures are of the same form, their appearance is not the same, but the relationships among the parts of one structure are similar to the relationships among the parts of the other (Gordon 1978, pp.40–44).

Another good example can probably be found in anti-oppressive practice. Within this orientation, groupworkers strive to prevent the relationship they have with group members from resembling oppressive relationships that members experienced in the past. Examples of these are when we see to it that no white worker is put in a position of repeatedly disciplining black persons, as this may replicate discriminatory practices in some schools, or when we ensure that the worker does not preach morality to young members of a group as this may be a structure that is parallel to practices in some oppressive families. Some groupworkers deliberately alter the power structure in the group so that it does not replicate the power structure from which group members suffered in the past. In systems terms, isomorphism is deliberately avoided.

Yet, for other purposes it is very helpful to draw on parallels; that is, to construct isomorphic structures. While drawing helpful parallels, group-workers can identify similarities and differences among a very large range of groupwork approaches. This is very much the purpose of the present inclusive stance. The attempt is not to force uniformity on practitioners, but to encourage diversity that can be articulated by drawing parallels to the essential elements of the paradox of talk: separating, connecting, and completing. Together, the three elements form a basic triangle that conveys the dynamics of capturing experiences in words.

The paradox of talk is the corner-stone. Parallel frameworks in which three aspects exist can be created provided the relationships among these aspects also involve separating, connecting, and completing. *Frameworks that involve these triangular dynamics will be described here as 'three-cornered worlds'.*

The major parallel to be drawn is with the relationship among contents, process, and structure as a three-cornered world.

Groupwork in a three-cornered world: Process, structure (levels) and contents

Having grounded the framework in the paradox of talk, the next stage is to create parallels to that paradox, and so ensure internal coherence of all the concepts. If the paradox of talk is the seed of this framework, then the first triangle may be likened to the roots. The roots from which groupwork grows are the group's dynamics, and these are seen here as a three-cornered world: a combination of process, structure, and contents, that are related to one another in the ways connecting, separating, and completing are related.

Group dynamics: process, structure and contents

Communication in groups gives rise to the group's dynamics, and these dynamics are of a three-cornered world. Here is how the three aspects of the dynamics are related to one another.

PROCESS

In every group there are moments when everybody talks at once, each interrupts the other, the topics change by the minute and nobody minds. The worker herself senses that something constructive is happening. She does not know what it is, but her intuition is to just let it be; to follow whatever is going on and find out later what, if anything, should be done.

When members resonate with one another, they experience mostly their relationships in the group – here and now, in the present. During these times members may interrupt each other, but they do so organically. A little gap appears in what someone says quite naturally. Then, as the message strikes a chord in another, she gives the conversation a little tilt, changing the subject somewhat but still somehow connecting. A third person comes in just when there is space. He has another angle which is also similar, and so it goes.

These here-and-now gestures, verging on the threshold of chaos, have no past and no future. They seem to be exchanged for the purpose of exchanging them; for sensing connections with others while separating from them. Spontaneously resonant moments among group members are precious and rather rare. Such periods of near-chaos have their own value in allowing members to sense closer affinity with one another and also the differences that render each person unique. In parts of the literature (Simon, Stierlin and Wynne 1985, pp.342–344), processes are not distinct from patterns and from structures. That view is a form of shorthand, and may prevent practitioners from responding to what Helen Durkin (1981) described as 'seemingly accidental and very fleeting emotions, thoughts, and actions' (Durkin 1981, p.188).

Strictly speaking, processes have no past and no future. Unpatterned, they emerge most purely in the present – these are the experiences that will never come back again. As Perls, Hefferline and Goodman (1951, p.33) put it: 'The wish to seize the present and pin it down – to mount it, as it were, like a butterfly in a case – is doomed to failure. Actuality forever changes.' This is why it is necessary to state explicitly that:

> *Processes are the constantly changing verbal and bodily influences among people in the present.*

SYSTEMIC SIGNIFICANCE

Continuously flowing processes are usually experienced as ever changing and freely mingling with one another. This is why it seems appropriate to see processes as parallel to the *connecting* aspect of the paradox of talk.

THE PROCESS OF FEEDBACK

Many influences are exchanged in the group. If we tried to handle all of them, we would probably have been swept away by the prevailing chaos. So, we select certain processes and ignore others. Systems theorists have selected feedback processes. This is not because the only processes that occur are feedback processes. It is simply because feedback processes have a considerable impact on mutual influences in the group. Feedback is relaying at least part of the reactions of the group back to it, or as James Durkin (1981, p.343) put it, feedback arises when 'part of the output…is returned as input'. Not everything that the worker says to group members is feedback. To be feedback, at least some part of the worker's statement must come from what group members have said in the first place.

Feedback is demonstrated in Figure 1.2 with an example. In this example, the session begins with a mute silence. The late adolescent members sit around and their faces convey very little. They look bored. Some members then say something related to having nothing to do. Others talk about another factory closing down in their borough. If the worker then suggests that members' boredom is related to them being unemployed ('rising unemployment is hard on you'), the worker is relaying at least part of the members' reactions to the situation back to them. The worker offers them feedback. Feedback must begin where the members are. The nature of feedback is presented in Figure 1.2.

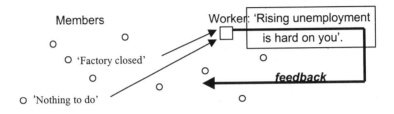

Figure 1.2 The process of feedback

Not all feedback processes are the same. In fact, it is possible to identify three different types of feedback and these will be described in Chapter 2, where the difference between phases and crises will be discussed.

By focusing on various feedback processes the worker can quickly gain access to a great deal of information about the potential for change in the group. Feedback processes are efficient (or in technical terms, parsimonious); though they may be few in number, they generate a great deal of information.

STRUCTURE

Relationships, as opposed to casual meetings, are rarely purely spontaneous one-off occurrences. This is why it is so difficult to understand relationships as pure processes. Certain processes are repeated in continuous relationships as they develop over time, and so 'redundancy' (Simon, Stierlin and Wynne 1985, pp.285–286) is established. It is more common to say that a *pattern* emerges. For example, the group session may begin only after the worker closes the door. At first, it does not matter who closes the door, as the act of closing the door is repeated every week to signal the beginning of the session. So, a pattern of closing the door is established whereby the door being closed is always followed by the start of the session.

When, in addition to the pattern, power positions are established, a *structure* is formed. An updated review of group structure was offered by Rohde and Stockton (1994). Resorting to the present example, if the door is always closed by the worker we can assume that norms are established which give the worker the authority to close the door. Only the worker is empowered to signal that the group session is about to begin. A difference emerges: it gives the worker certain powers in view of her position as the group leader. This difference, or *separation*, also deprives the group members of the power to signal the start of the session. The members' inferior powers are defined by their position as group members. Such positions too are usually supported by norms that justify them.

> *A repeated pattern in which positions of power to influence others emerge is a structure.*

SYSTEMIC SIGNIFICANCE

To identify structural differences, it is necessary to make a distinction between one sub-system and another. For example, such a distinction emerges when we identify part of the group as 'dominant' and the other as 'submissive', or when we look at the group as a whole and identify it as 'split up' compared to another which we see as 'cohesive'. The comparison introduces a separation: between sub-groups as in the first example, or between whole groups as in the second. Making distinctions always brings out the separating aspect of the paradox of talk. Therefore, all structural arrangements emphasise the Separating aspect.

THE IMPORTANCE OF LEVELS

As pointed out, structural arrangements introduce a *separation* within the group. Some topics and experiences are accepted as 'relevant'. These are separated from those which are considered 'irrelevant'. For example, in some groups, politics are considered to be a very appropriate topic for discussion but sexual intimacy is seen as irrelevant and even inappropriate. In other groups the opposite applies. The relevance or irrelevance of each topic may also change as group members learn more and more about each other over time. The groupworker needs to understand the dynamics of such separation. Without such understanding, a worker may push for disclosures that, at a certain stage, group members consider inappropriate. An example can be to enhance disclosures about sexual experiences while the group is engaged at the social level of struggling with trust, respect, and empowerment.

At another point, the groupworker may actually miss important issues; for example, she may fail to sense that a generalised social discussion about the merits of marriage is actually a prelude to a member's wish to explore her own feelings about getting married just a little later.

Pitching responses appropriately can be helped a great deal by gauging the level at which the group works at each point in time. The level emerges as the group settles for a certain consensus about the boundaries of expressions. Politics is 'in' or 'out'; religion is 'acceptable' or 'too personal', and so on. The group erects a boundary around issues and defines these as 'relevant', or 'appropriate'. These 'acceptable' issues are separated from others, which are then construed as 'irrelevant' or 'inappropriate'. Durkin (1981) called this ability to open and close boundaries, simply 'boundarying'. Boundarying leads to the creation of sub-systems, and each sub-system is always part of a larger set of boundaries, called 'supra-system'. Following Kantor and Lehr (1975), three typical sub-systems will be highlighted here. For the present purpose, I shall simply call them 'levels'. Because levels are meaningful human experiences, every level can be seen as a hologram – each contains within itself all the three aspects of the paradox of talk. Within each level, people separate issues from one another, connect these to one another, and complete the picture to render that level meaningful. Yet, over time, it is possible to see that one of the aspects of the paradox of talk is emphasised more strongly than the other two within each level.

These emphases will be explored now:

PERSONAL LEVEL

Most immediately and acutely, we experience the personal level. Even before we are able to find any words to convey our experiences we already sense coldness, warmth, tightness, and relaxation. These sensations pulsate inside our bodies and other people can see some indications of the fluctuations involved through our bodily gestures.

Indeed, for a while a group may choose to concentrate on each individual regardless of the accumulative effects of their relationships with others. Sometimes this is the focus of individual psychology. Focusing on individual differences, it is possible to explore idiosyncratic tastes, individual sensibilities, unique individual beliefs, or even the particular ways this person associates present experiences with memories of the past.

The personal level, and each person within it, can be conceived as a system too, particularly if Fairbairn's object relations theory is translated into systems terms (Manor 1992). It is then possible to explain why personal experiences are often so diffuse and confusing. Within the personal level each experience easily flows into another: fear quickly transforms into anger, sexuality and intimacy easily merge into one, dependency may be confused with religiosity. As this book will not include an extensive exploration of the psychodynamics of the personal level, I shall not expand on these dynamics here. The main point is that:

> *The Personal level is concerned with the influences among people with regard to their individual differences.*

SYSTEMIC SIGNIFICANCE

It is not a mere chance that psychoanalysis has concentrated on the personal level first. At the personal level we easily merge physiological, emotional, and cognitive functioning. Our memories can easily cloud our perception of what is happening in the present, and when memories are repressed their powers can easily confuse each individual. This inherently fluid nature of our internal worlds is also a rich source of images, fantasies, and creative solutions. In both senses, the personal level is usually seen as ever flowing, formless and diffuse.

> *This is why it makes sense to see the personal level as emphasising the Connecting aspect of the paradox of talk.*

RELEVANCE TO PRACTICE

For the present purpose, it is important to note that people need to feel free of pressure if they are to explore personal matters fully. The relevant differences of inclinations, private associations, and intimate beliefs cannot be simply

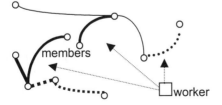

Figure 1.3 A loose structure for the Personal level

and directly ordered to appear. To explore them, a degree of spontaneous expression has to be encouraged in the group. Connections that are unexpected have to be allowed, and pre-determined boundaries that too easily separate one experience from the other would not be the priority. Therefore, a relatively loose structure, with no clear centre and with many opportunities to cross boundaries in many different directions, seems to be conducive to explorations at the personal level. This structure is conveyed in Figure 1.3 above.

INTERPERSONAL LEVEL

Most people find it very difficult to live only in the personal level all the time. Loneliness can be intensely painful and can even lead to mental health difficulties. In addition, joining forces with other people can offer each person strength that no person can have alone. Most people contain their personal level within a certain social arrangement, and this arrangement will be discussed a little later.

Focusing on the social level may lead to placing individuals in certain roles: male versus female, black versus white, gay versus heterosexual. Opening up the personal boundaries may lead to highlighting uniqueness of each person; whether male or female, black or white, gay or heterosexual. Most people tend to seek a combination of the two levels. This is why people often say, 'As a parent, I myself feel that …', or 'As an older adult, it is important to for me to …'. When people express these statements they offer a personal interpretation of their social positions, as they weave the two levels – the personal and the social, into one. People do create their own versions of the social roles allocated to them. Often personal politics and social psychology are dedicated to exploring such combinations. In general:

The Interpersonal level is where social roles are charged with personal meaning.

SYSTEMIC SIGNIFICANCE

When we resort to interpersonal statements such as 'As a parent I feel that …', or 'As an older adult it is important for me to …' we send a particular message to others. The underlying message is not always openly stated but it is usually quite clear. Usually such ways of expressing ourselves are strategies that allow us to claim the legitimacy of certain restraints in view of a certain understanding. The strategy is to refer, although without saying so, to a socially agreed norm. These norms are supposed to tell us what being 'a parent' is, what 'being an older adult' is, and so on. At the same time, such interpersonal frames also signal that there are issues that others – those who are not 'parents' or not 'older adults', may well not understand. By putting a social frame around personal issues we usually also erect boundaries beyond which others should not reach.

When conversations cross these boundaries, we can always say: 'Ah, this bit is too personal, I'm talking here as a (parent, older adult, and so on)'. This double edge of interpersonal relationships is probably their attraction. By resorting to the interpersonal level we can talk about certain issues that are important to us, while preventing the conversation from reaching those issues that are too painful or confusing for us. The interpersonal level provides us with the tools for regulating the distance between us and other people.

In this sense the Interpersonal level emphasises the Separating aspect of the paradox of talk.

RELEVANCE TO PRACTICE

Thinking about the interpersonal level structurally leads to preferring a certain type of group structure too. At the interpersonal level, members explore their own ways of assuming social roles. Therefore, each member needs to compare experiences with others. Usually members need opportunities to talk with one another more, and talk with the groupworker less.

The structure of a network, where lines of interaction cross one another in many directions, seems to be relevant to this level. Yet, members who explore interpersonal issues do not necessarily want to share more intimate individual and personal experiences in the group. They often want to control their expression quite deliberately. So, the group often needs the groupworker to

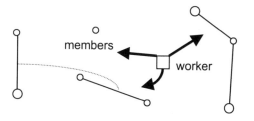

Figure 1.4 Network structure for the Interpersonal level

help in maintaining the boundaries against too personal intrusions. Therefore, when the interpersonal level is important to members, the groupworker may adopt a slight degree of centrality, so she can intercede on behalf of those whose personal boundaries seem to be invaded. This can be seen in Figure 1.4 on the previous page.

SOCIAL LEVEL

It is quite possible to focus on the ways people influence one another beyond the differences among them. This is often the focus of sociology: what all people between the ages of 14 and 18 years have in common; what all men have in common; what all women share: these questions draw the most comprehensive frame around people. Of course, no group is an island. By identifying some people as 'teenagers' or as 'men' we also say that there are other people who are not teenagers and not men. As we refer to those who are not inside the chosen frame of 'teenagers' or of 'men', we are bound to ask also what those outside the frame have in common with those who are inside. In this example, all those outside are 'human beings'. Once we reach the point of looking at all human beings we may well realise that other beings around us are here too but these are not human beings; these are animals.

Such acts of extending our frame can go on forever. The point is that once individual differences are excluded, we are potentially reaching out to the infinite totality of the universe. Quite a number of people involved in environmental issues are committed to extending our awareness in this way.

In many groups it is sometimes helpful to draw a frame around certain issues and ask how the accumulative effects of the mutual influences among people add up to throw new light on the plight of that group; for example, of women. In such a case, we would be concerned only with the characteristics that all women share, and ignore the differences among them. We can also ask how these accumulative effects make these people, for example women, different from another group, for example, men. We are then interested in what separates women from men, but we still ignore individual differences among women.

The Social level is the accumulative influences among people beyond individual differences among them.

SYSTEMIC SIGNIFICANCE

Infinitely extending our experience of living – potentially to the outer bounds of the universe, has a powerful impact. Among others, the impact is the all-embracing feeling of being *contained* within a frame that is far larger than any individual can fully comprehend. In this sense the social level is a very powerful container.

From a systems point of view, the containing Social level emphasises the Completing aspect of the paradox of talk.

RELEVANCE TO PRACTICE

In groupwork, there are times when the group is engaged mainly at the social level (in Chapter 2 these stages will be identified quite specifically). During these periods the structure known as a wheel may be quite helpful. This structure is pictured in Figure 1.5.

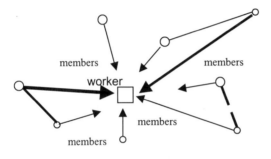

Figure 1.5 Wheel structure for the Social level

Within the group structure of the wheel the groupworker is central as she co-ordinates most of the influences. Members tend to address her most of the time, and relate to one another only very intermittently. Their interactions form a parallel arrangement, like the spokes of a wheel, around the group-worker. The advantage of this structural arrangement is that the members' openness with one another is relatively limited. Each talks to the worker only about the issues each member chooses to bring up. The worker, in turn, can stop each member, and so moderate the level of disclosure. As a result, group experiences are often that of being contained. At the same time, the exchanges usually include fewer surprises and less spontaneity too. In particular, more personal issues are less likely to emerge through the wheel arrangement because social arrangements create a container that includes putting a lid on very personal revelations.

Altogether, groups may fluctuate over three levels: Personal, Interpersonal and Social. For each level a different structure may be particularly helpful. Together, the three-cornered world of structure will appear as in Figure 1.6.

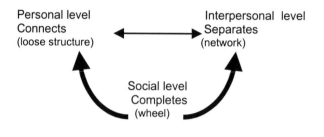

Figure 1.6 Structure as a three-cornered world

The built-in question: Process and structure in the group

It is misleading to focus on the structure alone. The reason is probably that structural levels are never totally divorced from the processes that mobilise them. For example, the worker who facilitates the structure of the wheel at the social level needs also to mobilise certain processes such as encouraging the members to listen to one another. Without the appropriate process this wheel may not, so to speak, revolve for very long as no member may feel sufficiently engaged in the experience as a whole.

Indeed, the debate between proponents of process-oriented and structured approaches to counselling and therapy has a long history (Rogers and Skinner 1956). Yet, the systems understanding is that the tension between the two is inevitable. This is so because one cannot be meaningfully sustained without the other (Sluzki 1983). Consequently, it is not really viable to talk about purely 'process-oriented' groups (for example, Brandler and Roman 1991), or about entirely 'structured' ones (Stockton, Rohde and Haughey 1992). Each group is a distinct combination of the two aspects.

The question is, of course, how we manage the inevitable tension between process and structure. Workers can influence the particular blend of process and structure in each group, and alter this blend during each group's development. As they do so, workers exercise some judgement about the desirable combination.

One way of exercising such judgement is by considering the dilemmas that pre-occupy group members. These dilemmas can be heard in the *contents* of group members' conversations.

Contents

How can a groupworker choose the appropriate level, and further on – within each level, how can the most relevant process be identified? These are crucial turning points to which groupworkers may have to respond. As noted at the very beginning of this book, many factors have to be considered: theory, practice experience, and research have to inform the worker all the time. Yet, these sources of knowledge are neither complete nor stable – many questions have been and probably will remain unanswered, and the answers that we do have may well continue to change.

So, in addition to this type of knowledge, personal values will have to continue to guide each practitioner. This is why worldviews are an important aspect of groupwork practice. Worldviews contain moral values that transpire through the contents of members' conversations, particularly in dilemmas with which they struggle.

The contents tend to appear in layers. The words are one layer, but the tone of voice and the bodily posture are also an important layer. A simple example of such layering will do. People in English-speaking countries use the phrase 'thank you very much' in rather different ways. A person saying this phrase while facing the other and smiling usually conveys gratitude, while when that person says the same phrase while turning away from the other and frowning, the message is that of anger. Therefore it is probably worthwhile noting that:

> *Contents are the combinations of bodily and verbal messages communicated by each person.*

To explain the present approach to contents, let us proceed in small steps. As the groupworker listens to the group, she hears their voices: words are uttered, and the words build up to sentences. How does the worker choose the expressions that call for her response? Cohen and Smith (1972) have influenced many groupworkers in this respect (see Pawlak and LeCroy 1981 for an example). The trained worker does not merely listen to *what* group members say; she also listens to *how* they say it.

Most people know the difference between talking and saying something. Talking is merely uttering words. While talking, words are expressed, but all of them sound the same: the voice remains the same and the body gestures are uniform. Such utterances are made without special involvement by the person producing them. Utterances contain very little information about that person's own experiences.

Speech acts

The worker can wait until a certain word or a phrase deviates, as it is such a difference that provides emotional information. Suddenly a person's voice quivers, or rises, or sinks to a whisper. Suddenly a difference appears. It does not matter at first what this difference is; the point is that emotional information is forthcoming. These deviations beyond the mere uttering of words are emotionally charged, and so carry more important messages. Emotionally charged expressions that deviate from a person's habitual way of speaking constitute speech acts. Speech acts provide new information about the person's involvement.

Themes

The trained worker pays special attention to speech acts. Having noticed them, the worker can go back to the words members have used, and ask herself: What do they all have in common? What are members saying during these special moments when they depart from their accustomed way of talking? Are these deviations related to authority figures, to loved partners, to children, to poverty? The possibilities are endless, but the rule seems to stand. More often than not, these exceptions add up to a theme; people do not usually deviate from the norms randomly. If, for example, many of the symbols and ideas expressed during these special moments are related to people who have power over group members, it is likely that most group members are now preoccupied with the theme of authority.

A theme conveys the concerns of the members by connecting speech acts that are distinguished from mere utterances.

In the present context, speech acts seem at first isolated; they give rise to the emphasis on Separating. With emerging themes, the emphasis on Connecting surfaces.

Yet, each worker needs to find a way of weaving speech acts into themes. The connections among speech acts cannot be established empirically very confidently. Practitioners usually say that they find the connections intuitively. I think that, on further reflection, most practitioners would agree that they rely on their sensitivity to moral dilemmas with which group members may struggle. The moral dilemmas are usually reflected in the contents of conversation; as principles, as symbols, as expressed aspirations and so on. So, it is to dilemmas that we have to turn our attention now.

Dilemmas

More often than not, dilemmas are grounded in moral issues and lead to articulating certain worldviews. These worldviews guide us in our daily affairs. Moral judgement also guides the worker in deciding how to blend process and levels. In this sense, moral views contain our actions and thereby bring forth the emphasis on the Completing mode of communication.

Altogether, the three-cornered world of contents can be charted as in Figure 1.7.

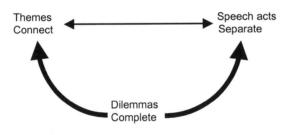

Figure 1.7 Contents as a three-cornered world

Many practitioners have contributed to the subject of ethics, morality, and worldviews. Just within the area of groupwork alone, volumes have been written – readers may be familiar with the work of Brammer, Abrego and Shostrom 1993; Brown 1992; Butler and Wintram 1991; Corey, Corey and Callanan 1993; Davis and Proctor 1989; Mistry and Brown 1997; Mullender and Ward 1991; or Sue and Sue 1990. Differences as well as similarities among practitioners can be discerned. The priority of genuineness between practitioners and group members, as well as among group members themselves, is probably clear throughout all groupwork approaches.

A fair and just distribution of power has been recognised as an important principle too. Commitment to and responsibility for other people is recognised, though interpreted in quite a number of different ways. The protection and active enhancement of minority rights and the need to understand clients' values that are different from those of the practitioners have been promoted with vigour.

Another value judgement underlies the present particular framework. The value is in *the powers of paradox.*

To appreciate the powers of paradox it is necessary to fully understand its nature. Paradoxes involve tension between opposites that inevitably lead to one another, and can be fully understood only when a hidden third dimension is unearthed to render both necessary (Rosenbaum 1982; Smith and Berg 1987). This is why the paradoxical relation between Separating and Connecting has been elaborated, and the parallel paradoxical tie between process and structure has been highlighted. When we choose to sustain a paradoxical position we find ourselves fluctuating between the polarities involved; for example, between process and structure, or between the personal and the interpersonal levels. The point is that by accepting a paradox as inevitable, we also undertake to shuttle to and fro between opposing polarities. Such fluctuations are a matter of choice. Clearly, not all tensions, contradictions, and strife are experienced as beneficial. Yet, some tensions are seen here as positive experiences.

One day we may know which paradoxical ties are not actually conducive to well-being and work to resolve them. Yet, some paradoxical experiences seem to me to be virtually life-enhancing. A good example is the relationship between structure and process. The value judgement behind working with the fluctuating system is that the practitioner should not try to resolve to be either 'facilitative' or 'structured'. Instead, the practitioner can sustain the paradoxical tension between the two, and let the group fluctuate over time so that each aspect may help members meet different needs at different stages.

Summary

In this chapter, concepts that might help groupworkers clarify the choices they made in practice were explored by focusing on the internal dynamics of the group. Perhaps it would be helpful to summarise the main points raised so far.

- Groupwork as a whole is so diverse that it is very difficult to compare and contrast practice let alone improve it.

- A unifying set of concepts is needed so that fragmented instances of practice are connected to one another.

- Practice that will be discussed here will include only time-limited groups where the focus is on interpersonal concerns and where there is commitment to increasing awareness of the relationships among group members.

- Furthermore, only the basic dynamics of working with such groups will be explored – leaving each worker to find the methods that fit the expected dynamics best.

- The proposed framework will be a version of the systems approach where communication is seen as the connecting thread revolving around the paradox of talk.

- The importance of the paradox of talk emerges when parallels to that paradox can be identified.

- Parallels to the paradox of talk are three-cornered worlds and the most important for the present purpose is the triangle of process, structure and contents. This three-cornered world is group dynamics.

- Furthermore, each of the three corners of group dynamics is itself a three-cornered world.

- Processes include three types of feedback and these will be discussed in Chapter 2.

- Structure comprises three levels: social, personal, and interpersonal.

- Contents are identified in three layers: speech acts, themes and dilemmas.

- Important dilemmas are hidden behind certain themes and these are handled by resorting to moral judgement.

- One of the moral positions behind the present framework is that certain dilemmas cannot and perhaps should not be resolved. Indeed, some dilemmas; particularly that of sustaining the inevitable tension between process and structure, may be life-enhancing.

CHAPTER TWO

Stages in a Three-Cornered World

'Destiny and freedom are engaged to one another.'

Martin Buber (1963)

The ideas developed in Chapter 1 are expanded in this chapter to construct an inclusive blueprint of group stages. Here is a summary.

First, the problems left unresolved by existing schemes of group stages are discussed. Then features that many schemes of stages have in common are identified. It is suggested that a systems view of group stages may resolve the problems mentioned before. The systems view of group stages is that the group changes from one stage to another according to group members' needs to open and close their boundaries. This ability to negotiate the openness of boundaries between group members and the worker, as well as among group members, is seen as vital and is called 'boundarying'.

When we understand the boundarying needs of group members we can see how group stages evolve within the three-cornered world of the group's structure. The feedback processes that enable such boundarying are then explained. These changes are of two types: incremental and transformational. The stages themselves fluctuate between periods of incremental changes which are called 'phases' and periods of transformational changes that are experienced as 'crises'.

These ideas are then used to articulate the communication cycle as comprising eight stages of group development. These eight stages are not expected to appear in all groups. The eight stages are merely the potential – the inclusive blueprint from which each group can construct its own stages according to its own needs.

The discussion will be structured within the following headings:

Prescribed, basic and evolving frameworks

Converging features

A systems view of group stages

Boundarying and group stages

The communication cycle

Fluctuations: phases and crises

Towards an inclusive blueprint

Evolving frameworks: the binocular view

Prescribed, basic and evolving frameworks

Rather like the sea, relationships ebb and flow – constantly revealing different aspects as time goes by. How can the worker know which of these aspects are most vital for group members at each point in time? Is this the time to focus on trust? Is it most important to pay attention to the competition among group members? That reference to sexuality, just made by one member, should I encourage further exploration now, or should I wait with such matters for later on?

Every groupworker struggles with these questions every time she works with a group. Most groupworkers do not rely only on their intuition when choosing how to respond. Usually the worker responds according to two major questions. One is whether the issue is relevant to this group. The other is whether most members are ready to share the exploration of this particular issue at this particular point in time. The relevance of each topic – trust, power, sexuality, and so on, is decided according to the goals of the group. Each group is set up to explore certain issues more than others, and the focus should ideally be related to these goals. The order of exploring each of the relevant issues is another matter. If the worker believes that each issue is best explored when most of the members feel emotionally involved and sufficiently safe to share the exploration, then the worker will influence the order of topics according to the group's dynamics.

How do we know the basic dynamics of each group? In Chapter 1, the dynamics were described as combinations of process, structure, and contents. These combinations keep changing as the group develops its relationships. Perhaps a metaphor may help in clarifying this. Imagine being in the middle of the ocean – how would you steer your way? How would you choose to turn right here and left there? Well, you would want to carry a map that charts the major directions in advance. Without that you may well be lost – easily rowing round in circles. Something like this is involved in working with groups. The worker needs an overall map – a general description of the directions in which this group may steer its own way through the relevant relationships. The worker also need some signposts – general markers that indicate the possible order of approaching each issue. These signposts have been called 'group stages'. A framework that will help you identify group stages will be proposed in this chapter.

As already pointed out, at certain points during the life of each group, the contents, processes, and levels coalesce. When these aspects converge meaningfully they are usually called 'a stage'. One of the major points of this book is that each group may develop through different stages. So, one way of distinguishing one group from another is by comparing the stages through which each group develops.

Indeed, stages of group development have been studied extensively (Lacoursiere, 1980), and Anderson (1984, p.65) reports on virtually hundreds of schemes. Most of these schemes can be called 'prescribed'. These frameworks are complete prescriptions of all the stages through which each group should develop. The assumption underlying prescribed frameworks seems to be that unless all the stages have been worked through, the group may not achieve all its goals. On the face of it, such prescriptions make sense. Yet, each of these prescriptions seems to be appropriate for a different group in a different context. No single framework seems to be adequate for all groups. As mentioned in Chapter 1, the results can be quite puzzling: as a supervisor and assessor, I have come across explanations that seem to impose prescribed stages on groups that do not show these stages, and indeed do not seem to need them when group members' goals are examined. One cannot help wondering whether practitioners realise that each framework was developed to pursue different clients' needs in a different setting. Furthermore, even when prescribed frameworks are adequate, they may still remain isolated from one another, and so it may not be possible to compare them to one another. Isolated designs can encourage the fragmentation of groupwork, and consequently the loss of mutual learning among groupworkers.

Another common solution is to refer only to the basics of group development; that is to the beginning, the middle, and the end, as Toseland and Rivas (1984) did. Yet, such a solution does not really overcome the problem, because the middle periods of different groups may vary considerably. The result is rather similar: closer comparison of the dynamics of each group, and thereby mutual learning among groupworkers, may be thwarted.

Yet, some helpful indications have emerged from prescribed frameworks, as these have converged upon certain features. These features will be the starting points of the present framework too.

Converging features

Interestingly, among the various approaches to time-limited groups, some aspects do appear similar to one another.

Two leading textbooks are good examples: one is in the work of Corey (1995), and the other in that of Brammer, Abrego and Shostrom (1993).

Both Corey (1995, pp.84–85) as well as Brammer, Abrego and Shostrom (1993, pp.383–243) arrive at four stages that are quite similar.

- The first stage is concerned with orientation to the whole experience of the new group.

- The second stage is about power issues.

- During the third stage, affective and intimate issues are explored.

- The fourth stage is dedicated to drawing lessons from the whole experience and applying them to daily life.

Levine (1979, pp.65–89) offers a rather penetrating exploration of the history of finding these stages. In the end, he himself develops a model that, in one respect, is quite similar to the consensus mentioned before. The similarity concerns Levine's phases: his *Parallel phase* is similar to the first orientation stage mentioned above; his *Inclusion phase* deals with power relations among peers; his *Mutuality phase* is indeed about mutual identification and closeness among members; and his *Termination phase* is focused on drawing lessons and preparing for life without the group.

However, Levine's explanation (1979) is offered within ego-psychology, as developed by Erik Erikson. Levine (1979, p.69) sees group development as a 'recapitulation of individual development'. Individual development is conceived as climbing up a ladder. Each step is higher up and each requires accomplishing all the previous ones. People cannot gain autonomy before establishing trust, and cannot properly cope with shame and doubt before they have secured enough autonomy (Levine 1979, pp.71–73). Such an understanding is usually called 'the epigenetic principle'. Levine's view is that the group too develops according to this principle. The group reflects individual emotional growth through its own developmental stages. In this sense, Levine's is one of the most prescribed schemes. It is true that Levine's scheme may suit some groups, but will it match the needs of all groups?

Anybody reviewing current journals in which papers about groupwork appear, will not fail to see that the various groups are designed to meet very different client needs. Indeed, very few of these groups aim to complete the full course of emotional growth prescribed by Erikson's model.

In group psychotherapy, the work of MacKenzie (1997) stands out in this respect. While adopting the above four stages as a starting point, MacKenzie advocates modifying the initial scheme to meet the needs of different psychiatric patients. The only limitation of MacKenzie's approach is that his psychotherapeutic framework may not be detailed enough to account for the very wide range of needs met through groupwork. It seems to me that the systems approach can retain the comprehensive nature of Levine's model yet interpret it in a far more flexible fashion so that it can be used to meet very different client needs.

This is also why some of the names Levine gives to certain stages will be altered. Levine's Parallel phase will be called here *'the Engagement phase'*, and his Inclusion phase will be called *'the Empowerment phase'*.

A systems view of group stages

The present systems approach to group stages is neither to prescribe complete schemes nor to encourage unbridled eclecticism. Instead, the intention is to encourage what might be called 'inclusiveness'. Within this stance, each practitioner is encouraged to evolve her or his particular framework of stages, while ensuring that all frameworks are derived from the same common pool. To create this common pool, an inclusive framework of stages is needed, and this chapter will deal only with its principles. The stages themselves will be demonstrated in Part 2.

The common pool will be explored now as grounded in an inclusive communication cycle. This cycle will emerge out of synthesising many sources, but I shall not mention each separately so as not to inhibit reading too much. Of course my own practice experience has informed the following discussion. If I had to single out three most influential sources, I think these will have to include Levine (1979) for his detailed description of group experiences during each stage, Durkin (1981) for the systemic explanations provided for many of these experiences, and Flemons (1991) for synthesising these explanations down to the basics of conscious communication.

As explained in Chapter 1, systems thinking begins by assuming that we communicate all the time: being in the world is communicating. Focusing on communication, systems theorists look at relationships rather than isolated bits and pieces of behaviour. From this basic position, other ideas have been developed, and these were explained in Chapter 1. There it was suggested that various systems could be explored as 'three-cornered worlds'. At the centre of this world we *connect* experiences by letting *processes* flow. At the same time, we also *separate* experiences by drawing distinctions and repeating these distinctions until a *structure* arises. This polarised tension between connecting and separating is grounded in a third aspect: often embedded in the *contents* of members' conversations. This aspect *completes* the picture; charging the other two modes with a particular meaning. The triangular relationship among process, structure and contents defines each group's dynamics. Figure 2.1 is a reminder of this basic position.

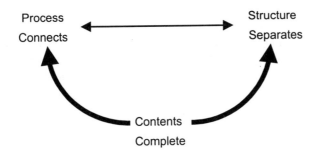

Figure 2.1 Group dynamics as a three-cornered world

Within this three-cornered world, identifying a group stage can be understood as separating various experiences from one another. Making a distinction between one stage and another, the group opens up its boundaries to certain dynamics; for example, to the dynamics of power. By doing so, the group also excludes different dynamics; for example, ones concerned with intimacy. As already mentioned, such opening and closing of boundaries is called by Durkin (1981) 'boundarying'. Therefore, the present analysis will begin by exploring more details involved in boundarying.

Boundarying and group stages

How do stages emerge in the group? To explore the answer, let me begin from the simple beginning.

As group members meet for the first time, they do not know what to expect and so, they concentrate on finding out. Group members compare other groups to the present one, and other leaders to the worker. First and foremost, they are trying to 'get the picture'; to sense the situation as a whole. In this sense, group members' communication can be viewed as focused on the mode of *completing*; charging the new situation with meaning.

How do group members discover the meaning of the new group? Some answers are often provided by the worker. These explanations are usually concerned with *the contents* as related to group members' goals. For example, in a parents' group, the worker may suggest that 'we shall probably talk about raising children (the contents) so you will not have to worry about harming them' (one goal). These explanations are helpful, but they leave some questions unanswered. Members may well ask: 'What about raising children? What will be considered relevant: personal hopes? Educational aspirations? Finance? So many aspects may be involved; at what *level* are we to explore each aspect here?'

Group members often test the appropriate level in various ways. One or two may divulge personal details, just to realise that nobody else is reciprocating. Others may begin to talk about situations they have just experienced with their own children. These disclosures are likely to be interpersonal, and even these may not be reciprocated by many group members very rapidly. More often, group members realise that they need first to find common ground; to establish what they all have in common over and above the differences among them. In the present example, the common ground may well be simply that of being parents.

Thus, at the beginning many groups focus on overall shared concerns. As explained in Chapter 1, these concerns are mainly at the *social* level; they arise over and above the differences among the individuals who form the group. You will see these dynamics described during the stage of Engagement in Part 2.

When enough of the members are assured that the rest, including the worker, are trustworthy and that all share some major concerns, members begin to form an attachment to the group and consequently begin to see it as different from other groups. In systems terms, the group begins to close its own boundaries. Some groups reach this stage very early, while others spend far longer periods on establishing their common ground. As group boundaries are closed, the internal dynamics of the group come to the fore – now members begin to experience how they affect one another. A different range of experiences is available to members – now they can explore how to go beyond purely socially prescribed roles, and infuse these roles with their personal interpretations. As explained in Chapter 1, this means that members can now explore *interpersonal* relationships.

As already explained, the interpersonal level has some distinct advantages: within this level each member can remain within a social role; for example, that of a parent, or of a woman. At the same time, each member can also express selected aspects of her personal world; her own preferences and her own priorities. Yet, each member can control such personal disclosures. Each can *separate* those personal aspects which she judges to be 'safe' from those she judges to be 'too threatening'. The member can create such a separation by referring to an agreed set of norms. Rather than having to say that she feels too threatened by a certain subject, the member can simply say: 'well, this is not really to do with being a parent'. The social role, of a parent in this example, can be used to draw the boundary around the personal issues that will be shared, and exclude those that will be kept at bay.

Usually, experiences at the interpersonal level emphasise competence and power relations more than openness and issues related to intimacy. The priority of power issues does not necessarily stem from members' judgement that only power issues are important to them. A different concern may be on members' minds: that of safety.

Why are power relationships experienced as safer than relationships that involve intimacy?

Power issues are often experienced as making distinctions between people: as more and less competent, or more and less helpful, and so on. Making such clear-cut distinctions is a way of separating experiences from one another. For example, the experience of being competent can be split from that of being incompetent. Then some people may be seen as most competent, while others may be branded least incompetent. In this sense, separating experiences from one another also means separating people from each other. The group may then divide itself between competent and incompetent members. A hierarchy of competence may be formed where everybody knows his or her place. With such an order established, the distance among group members can be readily regulated.

Armed with such means of regulating distance among themselves, members usually feel safe to begin to *connect* with one another more directly. In this sense, the separation ensured by focusing on competence and power at the interpersonal level provides the safest way group members have found in relating to one another at this stage. The dynamics of these relationships will be described as part of the Empowerment phase in Part 2.

Yet, in some groups, members' goals may lead them to realise that more intimate experiences also have to be explored. Some issues cannot be fully explored within the structured constraints of the interpersonal level. As a student suggested to me: 'you cannot make a contract to love'. This is why members are likely to approach the *personal* level. To use another metaphor, the personal level does not resemble a telephone switchboard. At this level it is not always possible to agree on switching on one issue and switching off another. For example, the search for mastery cannot always be separated from the drive to harm others; particularly when insecurity about one's own ability to cope with life has been threatened. Sexual attraction cannot always be separated from the wish to possess the other, particularly when one's confidence about being loved has been eroded. When members want to explore these experiences they often find the interpersonal level constraining. Members may then sense that to explore openness and intimacy the group has to be engaged at a different level; the personal one. However, the dynamics of the personal level are rather different from those regulated at the interpersonal level.

The personal level heightens connections of which we may not always be aware. At this level everything mingles with everything else: connections are formed, abandoned, and re-formed – sometimes very rapidly indeed. The personal level is experienced as a fluid narrative more than a clearly prescribed contract. In this sense, the continuous connectedness of personal experiences with one another highlights the *connecting* mode that evolves as we become aware that we communicate. Such connectedness will be conveyed when the phase of Mutuality is described in Part 2.

Personal explorations can last for quite a while. Yet, whether group experiences are focused on power issues, on intimate concerns, or on both, in time-limited groups the end is known in advance. So, as the end of the group approaches, members are likely to realise that these unique group relationships are not going to last forever. This is why members are likely to begin to detach themselves from the personal level. The personal level is abandoned because it is not likely to last. Instead, members prepare themselves for life after the group.

Towards the end, competition for power tends to diminish too. Power tends to lose its attraction – probably because members realise that whatever hierarchy has been formed it will soon be irrelevant. As the group reaches its end, its hierarchy will dissolve. So now, rather than jockeying for more power positions, members are likely to be busy reviewing the group experiences as a whole. Now they need to find out what lessons they can derive from their experiences and how these may be applied outside the group – in their daily life.

Outside the group, relationships are likely to be less personal. So, members are likely to focus on the interpersonal level again, and to some extent, on the social one too, but now they may well do so in view of the relationships that are external to their group. These dynamics will be explored when the Termination phase is described in Part 2. During that stage members tend to review their experience as a whole, and tend to focus on the *completing* mode. Such focus will charge the group experiences with an overall sense of meaning and link these group experiences with relationships outside the group.

If this explanation is valid, then group development can be understood according to communication needs of the members.

The communication cycle

As will be shown in Part 2, not all groups develop through all the stages that may possibly arise. Not all groups boundary all the levels of communication. Still, in order to secure coherence of concepts, it is necessary to gain a full view of all the possibilities first. The thread connecting all these possibilities is the communication cycle. Now this cycle can be identified.

The previous discussion suggests that members tend to start by emphasising the *completing* mode as they engage in orientating themselves towards the new group. They then focus on the *separating* mode; sorting out power positions to secure acceptable distance among themselves. Only later are members fully involved in the *connecting* mode. Yet, towards the end, members resort to the *separating* mode again. The members end where they began: stressing the *completing* mode to orientate themselves towards the outside world.

This abstract scheme may not be very helpful on its own. The value of this scheme emerges when we begin to draw parallels to these aspects of the paradox of talk. The parallels were already suggested, but these deserve summarising:

A parallel to *completing* can be found in the *social* level.

A parallel to *separating* can be seen at the *interpersonal* level.

A parallel to *connecting* can be discerned at the *personal* level.

Bearing in mind the parallels involved, you can see the communication cycle move within the three-cornered world of the structure; that is, through the levels of the group's dynamics. When the communication modes of the paradox of talk are matched to the various levels of the group's dynamics, the following connections appear:

- The full cycle begins when the group emphasises the *completing* mode at the *social* level.

- The cycle then moves on to stressing the *separating* mode at the *interpersonal* level.

- Further on, the dynamic shifts to focusing on the *connecting* mode as it enters the *personal* level.

- From the *personal* level the cycle begins to reverse its course: out of the personal level it shifts back to emphasising the *separating* mode at the *interpersonal* level.

- Often involvement at the *interpersonal* level then overlaps with emphasising the *completing* mode at the *social* level.

So, the fully inclusive cycle of group stages can be seen to evolve through all three modes of conscious communication as these serve the need for boundarying at all three levels of the structure.

This is why I call the course of group development 'the communication cycle'. In Figure 2.2 the two aspects: communication mode and structural level, are depicted together:

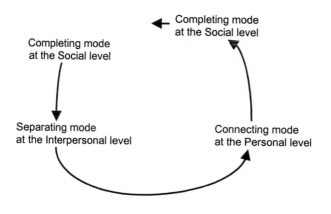

Figure 2.2 The cycle of communication modes through the group's levels

Still, a question remains unanswered even with this explanation. How do groups move on from one stage to the other? This is where Levine's model (1979) has a distinct advantage over many others. Levine distinguishes between two types of stages: one is 'phase', and the other is 'crisis'. As noted before, Levine's phases are congruent with the four commonly observed ones. His crises are periods of transition between the phases.

However, Levine does not provide a very detailed account of the different *processes* involved in each of these two types of stages. Both types are concerned with 'affective polarities' yet each seems to serve different purposes. From a systems perspective the dynamics of phases are markedly different from those of crises, and these will be explored now.

Fluctuations: Phases and crises

To understand the relationship between phases and crises, the processes involved have to be added to the levels. As explained in Chapter 1, within the systems approach, processes are forms of feedback. Three types of feedback can be identified. Although these feedback processes constantly mix and mingle with one another, it is easier to look at each separately, and in relation to the ways these appear during phases and in crises.

Phases

Levine writes that: 'A major feature of each phase is the directionality of relationships among the members and the therapist. In each phase the direction of relationship has distinctive characteristics not found in other phases.' (Levine 1979, p.73). This means that during the stage of group development called 'phase', members know and agree, at least tacitly, the purpose of the group and how to pursue it.

In their different ways each of the members works out the relationships that are relevant to following that direction, and usually they agree about the relevance of certain issues to the perceived purpose. For example, during the Engagement phase the direction may involve developing trust. During this phase, each member is mainly involved in working out how trustful she or he can be towards the others. During the Empowerment phase the direction may be to enhance a sense of competence. Then each member, again in her or his way, explores power issues and finds out how to handle the degree of power allowed in this group.

What does the systems approach have to add in this respect? Where Levine writes that 'the four phases represent the achieved directional and qualitative change in relationships' (Levine 1979, p.73), a systems theorist will add that once the direction is chosen, small, step-by-step, incremental changes can be worked out. Such incremental changes are introduced mainly through the process of stabilising feedback. What is involved in stabilising feedback?

STABILISING

To explain the process of stabilising feedback, let me begin with another example. In the middle of a group session, Jane is saying this, John is saying that, and Jeannie interrupts. The worker turns her head towards the rest of the group to see their responses. On the face of it, the process seems to just happen. Yet, a distinction is beginning to emerge. Jane, John, and Jeannie begin to appear different from the rest of the group: they appear to 'dominate' it. The worker then says: 'I wonder what other members feel about this?' When the worker makes such a comment, she is indeed responding to communication: verbal from Jane, John, and Jeannie, and bodily from the rest of the group. She is also relaying part of this communication: 'about this', back to the group. The worker is employing feedback, but which type?

To find out we must go back to the example. When you look at the interactions again, you can see that the groupworker was not just wondering. Presumably, that worker had judged that the domination of those three Js (Jane, John, and Jeannie) was less desirable than a full participation by more group members. So, the worker had already decided what would help the group; she had a predetermined level of activity on her mind prior to responding. When she responded, the worker was trying to bring the group to that predetermined level by taking the small step of asking for others' feelings.

In earlier times we would have said that the groupworker 'negated' the domination of the three Js; that the groupworker was offering 'negative feedback' (Simon, Stierlin and Wynne, 1985, pp.155–158). Negative feedback is not condemnation or telling off; it is going in reverse direction to an undesired 'deviation'. Nowadays it makes much more sense to say that the groupworker was compensating the group for the domination of the three Js, and so creating a pattern she considered desirable. Steering the group towards a desirable pattern tends to stabilise interactions within an expected range. This is why I shall refer to negative feedback simply as *stabilising*.

Stabilising redresses a certain balance the groupworker has on her mind. If all the members talked at once and could not hear one another, that worker would have probably judged that they all participated too much. If that was her judgement, she would have suggested that each spoke in turn for a while. Yet, decreasing members' participation in that way would have resulted from the same type of judgement: that there was an optimal level of involvement for that group at that point. So, decreasing participation, just like increasing it, would have been a form of stabilising too. This is shown schematically in Figure 2.3.

Whenever somebody in the group judges that there is a desirable range of influences and tries to bring the group to that range, 'stabilising' is employed.

Stabilising implies that we separate influences: distinguishing those which are within the desired range from those which are not. The steps taken towards the desired range are usually estimated one by one, to ensure that this range is neither missed nor exceeded. Therefore, stabilising is usually offered step-by-step; incrementally. 'I wonder what others feel?' may be the first step. If this response does not bring in other members, the worker may be more direct and say: 'Gill, Gerald, George – what do you feel?'

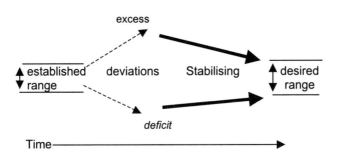

Figure 2.3 Stabilising: Reducing either excess or deficit

Because stabilising is offered in small steps it can be promptly reinforced. For example, once Gill, Gerald, and George speak, the groupworker may say, 'I am beginning to understand much more when more of us say what they think'. Such a response is a form of approval; the worker shows satisfaction immediately after change has occurred. By doing so, the worker is reinforcing the change and is increasing the likelihood that members will participate fully again. This is why cognitive-behavioural and all other structured approaches to groupwork can be seen to emphasise stabilising in their practice. This is also why the term 'incremental change' captures the process better than the previously established 'first order change'.

When such change is pursued, the result can increase separate skills; in our example, that of participating in small group discussion. Incremental changes enhance the members' competence in pursuing their chosen goal (Breunlin 1989). An example can be learning to choose a shared activity by going through the steps described in Figure 2.4.

While they increase their competence, the members and the worker already know where they are going – a pre-determined level is already on their minds. Therefore there is no need to change roles, rules, and norms that form the group culture – the point is to elaborate and consolidate these aspects.

Altogether, although different phases may evolve at different levels, all phases emphasise stabilising and during all phases incremental changes are pursued. In this sense, incremental changes contribute towards the continuity of the culture that is already available to the group.

The question then is how the group shifts focus: in the above example, how the transition is made from one phase to another – from exploring

power to exploring issues concerned with intimacy. This is where understanding crises is helpful.

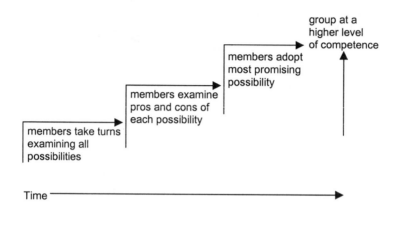

Figure 2.4 Problem-solving as step-by-step incremental changes

Crises

Levine (1979, p.73) continues by explaining that: 'The resolution of the
crises as they arise represents points of change in the directionality and
emotional quality of relationships'.

Crises, then, must be stages of turmoil; of simultaneously trying out
different directions, of considerable confusion, and of a great deal of
searching and anxiety. Yet, Levine describes the experiences of the group
during crises in more or less the same terms as those of phases. It is not clear
from his account that the dynamics are very different.

Where Levine (1979) writes that 'the recurrent crises represent changes in
the quality of relationships...' (Levine 1979, p.73), a systems theorist will
explain that 'the quality' emanates from changes in the roles, rules and norms
of the group. These 'points of change in the directionality and emotional
quality of relationships' (Levine 1979, p.73) have different dynamics and
involve different experiences. Family therapists have called such a change
'second order change' and have explained that a transformation is involved.

What do we know about transformational change? Transformational
change seems different from incremental change. Gergen (1982) explored
the process in broader terms. Leifer (1989) analysed how large organisations

go through transformation. Gemmill and Wynkoop (1991) have offered a psychodynamic understanding of small group transformation. The present understanding of transformation draws on all these sources, and adds a few more details.

During a phase the 'achieved directionality' is manifest in an agreement to remain within a certain range of behaviours. For example, during the Empowerment phase only issues related to the use of power, usually within a certain hierarchy, are allowed to be expressed. Usually, the norms – for example, that being powerful is good – are supposed to be accepted and members are also expected to express appreciation of this type of competence. Such a consensus is typical of a system's steady state; or 'homeostasis'. A crisis begins when someone deviates from the steady state.

In the present example, a member may say: 'I don't give a damn about being able to ...' (talk clearly, run fast, etc.). The member then defies the group's norms which direct her or him to appreciate competence. The group may react to this deviation in at least two different ways. One is to suppress it: to tell the member to shut up and toe the line. Such suppression involves a form of stabilising. If stabilising is attempted and is successful, the group remains in the same phase. The other possibility is that this deviating member is not alone in feeling indifferent about the use of power. Other members too may wish to share doubts, fears, and their struggle with failures. In such an eventuality, someone else may say: 'Right on! We've had enough of this rat race here.' If others join the fray, the initial deviation will be amplified. Amplifying is another form of the process of feedback, and it is useful to understand what is involved.

AMPLIFYING

Let me move on with the group example now. The groupworker had involved Gill, Gerald, and George (the three Gs) as much as Jane, John, and Jeannie (the three Js). There followed a period of joint problem solving, usually led by the worker. The members raised several specific issues on which they wanted to work: negotiating the right price in a shop; telling a stranger you have just met that you would like to see him or her again; responding to somebody who unexpectedly shouts at you; all could have been examples. The worker had been central in helping the members clarify and rehearse the skills involved and good work had been done.

Yet, that worker had been aware that Fiona and Frank had been far less involved, and their passivity had puzzled the worker. In the following session, another member raised another specific situation. Most of the members said that it was interesting and seemed settled to work on the issues awaiting the worker's prompt. Just as all seemed well, Frank and Fiona began to giggle between themselves. Most of the members reacted negatively to the pair; frowning and leaning forward towards those 'two Fs'. Gill even said, 'What's the matter with you two?', and George added, 'Look, if you don't want to work here, you can go elsewhere.' Clearly, by giggling, the 'two Fs' were deviating from the norms of 'work' developed by the group. The worker was then in a dilemma. She could see the two Fs as 'disrupting' the group's work and could treat them as deviants who had to be brought to order through group pressure. Indeed, the group, through Gill and George, had already begun to apply pressure by condemning the giggling of the two Fs. However, the worker was also aware of the peripheral and passive position adopted by the two Fs and was concerned about them. In addition she was increasingly uneasy about the group's norms, as the members continued to require that she lead all the skills learning sessions. A rather stifled atmosphere was beginning to develop.

In that situation, the worker ventured to look beyond the established right and wrong for a while. She decided to see the giggling not as a disruption and deviance, but as a message from Fiona and Frank, which was still not heard. The worker's first purpose was then to enable everybody to hear the message of the two Fs loud and clear.

Pausing for a while, the worker realised that she herself felt somewhat ridiculous being so central for so long. So much suggesting, teaching, and coaching made her feel like a football coach, or a cook; moulding members' behaviour. Having realised that, the worker smiled a little, and said: 'Well, to be honest, perhaps there is something funny here; I don't know.' This expression: 'there is something funny here' was *amplifying* the two Fs' initial deviation and relaying it back to the group in an intensified fashion. When the worker said so, she did not have any pre-determined form of participation in her mind. She just felt it was time to open up certain issues and guessed that the deviating giggle might lead to it. Fiona then burst out laughing, and said loudly: 'Come on, you do know, Miss.' The worker sensed a message was emerging, but was still unsure what it was. So, she said: 'Am I a Miss? Is it about me?' By inviting Fiona to say more, the worker was further amplifying the original deviation. Having done that, Frank responded angrily with: 'Well, you do act like one.'

Now, and only now, could the real issue come up in the open. It turned out that other members also had felt that the worker was treating them like school children and resented that. A demand from the members was growing that the worker let go of teaching them so much, and allow each of them to suggest what to do. The worker accepted that demand, and a period of negotiation followed, during which the group re-organised its ways of working.

The worker's response in this situation was markedly different from the one discussed under *stabilising*. The worker could have encouraged the members to pressurise Fiona and Frank to participate more in the group. Such a response would have been a form of stabilising. Yet, in our example, the worker did not do that. Instead, the worker temporarily suspended the act of judgement. For a while, she was not concerned with more or less participation. Rather, she was single-mindedly *amplifying* the deviation (the giggling) from the group's norms. Such an amplification was not pursued with any pre-determined level on the worker's mind; it was pursued for its own sake.

Earlier in the history of family therapy, this type of feedback was called 'positive feedback', not because it contained compliments and praise, but because it repeatedly increased the intensity of the electric charge. More electric charge was symbolised by the plus sign and called 'positive' (Hoffman 1981, pp.50–51; Simon, Stierlin and Wynne 1985, pp.33–34). The term had confused many, and soon 'deviation amplifying' took its place. For the present, it is enough to refer to the essence: intensifying a disturbing experience, or in short: *amplifying*.

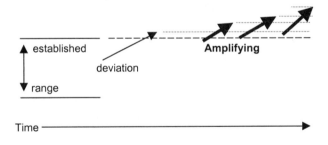

Figure 2.5 Amplifying

Amplifying is pursued when someone temporarily suspends the established moral judgement and persistently intensifies a deviation from the group's norms.

Unlike stabilising, amplifying tends to lead to a temporary sense of chaos when established distinctions between right and wrong are provisionally blurred. In this sense, amplifying draws on the connecting mode of communication. A crisis erupts when a certain deviation from the steady state is persistently intensified; so much so, that chaos prevails for a while. Then the whole system is temporarily thrown into increased confusion by the escalating impact of amplifying.

Many systems seem to propel themselves into a near state of chaos for a time (Gleick 1987; Fuhriman and Burlingame 1994; Prigogine and Stengers 1984). Indeed, periods of near total chaos seem necessary if certain changes are to emerge. People often cope with the eruption of chaos by splitting their experiences into two: the desirable and competent part, and the undesirable deviation. In the previous example the deviation of the two Fs was likely to be split from expressions of unrealistic fears for the worker's well-being and an exaggerated loyalty to the worker expressed by another minority. Yet, it is the deviation that is seen as 'the only problem'. As Breunlin (1989) showed, such splitting is evident while working with families too.

A systems practitioner sees the root of the problem not in the deviation, but in the underlying norms of the group that split experiences from one another. In this example, the problem is really the preoccupation of members with power to the exclusion of more personal and ambiguous issues related to intimacy. If the group is to find a new direction, it will have to commute these beliefs for more comprehensive ones. These new beliefs will have to be ones that enable interpersonal competence as well as personal intimacy. When such dynamics arise, new norms, rules, and roles are likely to follow. These changes lead to finding a new structure within which the members can more freely move between being interpersonally competent and personally intimate.

During crises Amplifying is emphasised and this emphasis usually leads to transformational change.

Transformational change has its own value. During the turmoil of this chaos, group members can re-examine their roles, rules, and norms, and revise them. This revision may also include the group's initial purpose. Resolving the crisis, members often combine the useful aspects of their 'competent' behaviours with the helpful, although modified, features of their deviation. So, the crisis often leads to broadening the range of experiences as well as the roles, which are acceptable within the group.

This is a rather broad description of transformational change, and I have proposed a somewhat more detailed model that occurs during the stage called the Authority crisis (Manor 1997). This crisis will be demonstrated in Part 2.

The general dynamics of crises are charted in Figure 2.6.

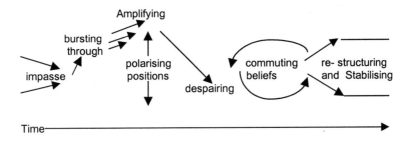

Figure 2.6 The full course of transformational change

It is not clear that all groups have to go through a crisis before entering every new phase. On the face of it, I would suggest that the evidence for such a generalisation is lacking. My own observation is that crises erupt more often in a less structured group and particularly when members experience *intense ambivalence* about entering a new phase. Members do seek the new range of experiences as much as they try to avoid that range. Only when such a degree of ambivalence prevails do crises erupt.

Therefore, if members are ambivalent about the role of the worker, they are likely to experience the *authority crisis* before venturing the *empowerment phase*. If members are ambivalent about revealing highly personal concerns they are likely to enter the *intimacy crisis* before they settle for the *mutuality phase*. If members are ambivalent about the ending of the group they may experience the *separation crisis* before arriving at the *termination phase*.

Examples of groups that do not show some or even any crises will be discussed in Part 2.

To summarise

During phases, stabilising is emphasised while incremental changes are pursued. The phases contribute to the continuity of the group's culture.

During crises, disturbing experiences are amplified and so transformational changes are possible. Crises alter the group's culture.

However, group members and their workers always need to make sense of their experiences – whatever these are. In most groups, explanations, and process commentary are offered. In some groups interpretations are added. '*Reframing*' is another form of clarifying that has been elaborated in family therapy. These processes of feedback are needed to expand the under-standing of relationships and render change meaningful. What is involved in *clarifying*?

CLARIFYING

Let us look again at the two examples. In the first, rather than asking members to respond, the worker could have said: 'Jane, John, and Jeannie are doing all the talking while the rest are standing by.' In the second example she could have said: 'Fiona and Frank are giggling and the rest of the group seems to be annoyed. I hope we can also talk about it all.'

In both instances, the worker would have been relaying the members' reactions back to them, and thus would have offered them feedback: she would have communicated part of the group's communication back to that group. Yet, that feedback would have been different from the previous two. Now the worker's comments would have drawn attention to a possible link between behaviours. In the first example she would have linked the domination by Jane, John, and Jeannie to the passivity of the rest; and in the second she would have linked the giggling of Fiona and Frank to the feeling of annoyance by the rest of the group.

Groupworkers usually call such responses 'process commentary': the worker observes what happens in the group and comments about a possible link between these isolated expressions. To do this the worker has to detach herself to some extent from the group, allowing the members' behaviours to impress themselves upon her so that she can clearly perceive the situation. When the worker feels comfortable enough to share her overview with the group, she communicates to the group *about* its communication; she does not direct the communication, as in stabilising, nor does she intensify it; which would have amounted to amplifying. Instead, the worker is suggesting a more complete picture. The worker is facilitating a shift of perception to a more comprehensive angle.

In family therapy communication about the communication has been called 'meta-communication' (Simon, Stierlin and Wynne 1985, pp.164–168). Yet, this expression does not make it clear that it is a form of feedback; nor does the term capture an important aspect of this feedback.

Whenever the worker links up bits and pieces of communication, she offers feedback; she does not just communicate. The worker selects a certain range of behaviours and then links them to one another.

Many things happen in the group at once. Domination and passivity is only one pair among quite a number of other possibilities. Of course, giggling and annoyance is another pair. Pointing out one link excludes others. The worker chooses which link to highlight at each point in time. She selects one link because she has reason to believe that it is this particular link which is most important at this particular moment for the group; she considers this particular link to be related to the 'problem' the group is facing now.

How does a worker choose the link she will highlight? Of course, knowledge, experience, and training help. Yet, the choice is also grounded in the worker's ethical and moral beliefs. For example, the worker may believe that domination is 'bad' as it stifles genuine relationships and 'causes' groups to stagnate. She may also believe that genuineness is 'good', and so, giggling is not a disruption but a message signalling the unexpressed need to be honest. A moral evaluation underscores both choices.

For a long time, systems thinkers have been intensely interested in unearthing the moral bases of such choices. They adopted the term 'punc-tuation' for the ways each party 'subjectively perceives different patterns of cause and effect' (Simon, Stierlin and Wynne 1985, p.284). Wilden (1980) used the term 'signifying' when he described the processes involved. In order to emphasise that I am dealing here not with abstract telegraphic codes but with significant human dilemmas, I shall retain the term many groupworkers know; that is, *'clarifying'*. Figure 2.7 illustrates the very first step of clarifying the instance of giggling mentioned above.

Clarifying is relaying to the group a possible link between at least two of their messages. This link charges members' experiences with additional meaning.

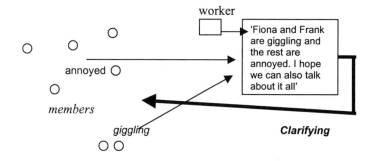

Figure 2.7 Example of Clarifying

SYSTEMIC MEANING OF CLARIFYING

What is the effect of the emerging meaning? From the present perspective, clarifying offers members the opportunity to experience and fully face inevitable dilemmas. The inevitable tension between the wish to belong and the need for autonomy, is one such dilemma. The unavoidable struggle between the wish to find our identity and the need to conform is another. Relationships are saturated with such seemingly impossible choices. As explained in Chapter 1, these dilemmas can be understood as emanating from an underlying paradox. A range of these paradoxes will be explored in Part 2 where each stage of group development will be characterised by certain dilemmas and the paradoxes underlying each. By its very nature, paradox is the way two mutually contradictory aspects inevitably lead to one another and, at the same time, are made meaningful by a third aspect that contains both. Clarifying tends to draw out this capacity of the Completing aspect to contain apparent contradictions. The tension between polarities becomes more manageable and even promising – as a source of new possibilities. When confusing aspects are clarified the relationship as a whole is more easily contained. This is how clarifying tends to bring out the Completing mode of communication during both crises and phases.

With these concepts in mind, it is possible to reflect on the interplay between phases and crises as in Figure 2.8.

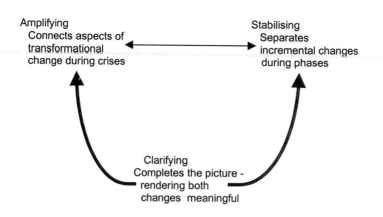

Amplifying
Connects aspects of
transformational
change during crises

Stabilising
Separates
incremental changes
during phases

Clarifying
Completes the picture -
rendering both
changes meaningful

Figure 2.8 The interplay between phases and crises as a three-cornered world

- Phases emphasise stabilising and contribute to incremental changes.

- Crises emphasise amplifying and lead to transformational alteration of the group's norms, rules, and roles.

- Clarifying is needed during both phases and crises so that the group can make sense of all the experiences, contain the tensions, and pursue its goals.

During the full communication cycle, both phases and crises are necessary. The reason is rather simple: the group, like any other system, has to achieve certain goals, and to do so the group needs some degree of continuity. Yet, in some groups, the goals are likely to change over time. When the goals have to be altered, the group itself has to change. Some of these changes cannot evolve without the group experiencing one of the crises. It follows that in such groups both are needed: the continuity of phases as well as the chaos of crises.

To paraphrase the initial quote from Buber: phases and crises are engaged to one another. The predictability of phase-like experiences (Buber's 'destiny') keeps alternating with the chaotic experiences of crises (Buber's 'freedom'). The more comprehensive the goals of the group, and the more ambivalent are members about entering each phase, the more members are likely to experience the full communication cycle, as depicted in Figure 2.9.

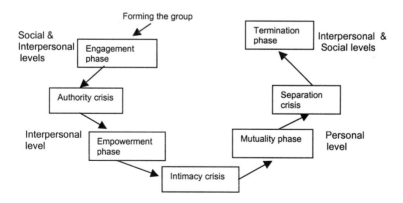

Figure 2.9 The full communication cycle

Towards an inclusive blueprint

The communication cycle is the skeleton of full-fledged group development. In a manner of speaking, flesh has to be put on these bones. The communication cycle will come to life when the contents of each stage are added. The contents will reveal the dilemmas and therein the paradoxes that underlie each stage. In Part 2, certain paradoxes will be identified for each stage and, together with certain levels and processes, these three corners will form the *inclusive blueprint of group stages*.

By way of introducing this blueprint, here are its stages.

Overview of the stages

Stage	Paradox	Process	Level
Forming the group (Ch. 3)	Involvement	Mainly Stabilising and Clarifying, mild Amplifying	Social
Engagement Phase (Ch. 3)	Trust and Reciprocity	Mainly Clarifying and Stabilising, slight Amplifying	Social to Interpersonal
Authority Crisis (Ch. 4)	Authority	Amplifying and Clarifying, weak Stabilising	Abandon Social to re-define Interpersonal
Empowerment Phase (Ch. 4)	Identity	Mainly Clarifying and Stabilising, no Amplifying	Interpersonal
Intimacy Crisis (Ch. 5)	Intimacy	First Amplifying, Clarifying, later Stabilising	From Interpersonal to Personal
Mutuality Phase (Ch. 5)	Regression and Creativity	Mainly Clarifying, some Amplifying, mild Stabilising	Personal
Separation Crisis (ch. 6)	Courage	Mainly Amplifying, active Clarifying, little Stabilising	From Personal to Interpersonal
Termination Phase (Ch. 6)	Dependency	Mainly Stabilising, active Clarifying, no Amplifying	Interpersonal and Social

To benefit from adopting the inclusive blueprint, the practitioner needs a certain perspective. A dual perspective is needed here: like figure and ground. The figure is the particular basic design chosen for a particular group. The ground is the inclusive blueprint; it is the range of possibilities out of which a particular design is chosen.

Evolving frameworks: The binocular view

Clarifying the particular course of each group's development requires a 'double description' (Keeney 1983, pp.37–44). As if holding a sophisticated binocular, the groupworker can keep the inclusive blueprint in mind all the time. This blueprint offers the full view of communication in groupwork. Yet, for each different group the worker can focus on only some stages of the inclusive blueprint and relegate others to the background.

Of course, all groups have to be formed, engage sufficiently, and end constructively. In terms of the present cycle: all groups have to begin with the stage of Forming the Group discussed in Chapter 3, they have to enter the Engagement phase demonstrated in the second half of Chapter 3, and they should end purposefully at the Termination phase, as demonstrated at the end of Chapter 6. Yet, in between these phases, each worker can choose to emphasise those phases and crises that best serve the members' goals. All these choices will be fully demonstrated in Part 2.

This evolving, rather than prescribed, view of group stages is possible without necessarily turning group experiences into mechanical sequences of artificially imposed stages. The genuine flow of experiences from one into the other may be possible because each of the stages already contains the same basic aspects. The fundamentals of communication: Separating, Connecting, and Completing, are already imprinted inside each stage. While each separate stage is likely to bring out these aspects in a different way, the ingredients are the same in all the stages. Therefore, each stage is also connected to all the others. Within this constellation, every combination is a different version of the same three-cornered world, and thus, each is likely to resonate with all the others.

This is the advantage of the holographic nature of evolving frameworks: it allows for a coherent common pool of stages, and also for evolving from that pool many different designs. In this way, many types of groupwork may be included in the same framework.

Summary

Perhaps it would be helpful to summarise the main points of this discussion.

- Stages are important as signposts of the ways relationships may develop in each group.

- Although many schemes of group stages have been developed, four stages have emerged as common.

- The four common stages can be found also in Levine's (1979) framework where these are called: the Parallel phase, the Inclusion phase, the Mutuality phase, and the Termination phase.

- Levine's (1979) framework is grounded in ego-psychology, which is a theory that may not be always helpful as it requires all groups to undergo all the stages.

- The systems view of stages is grounded in the need of group members to boundary their relationships.

- Based on the need to boundary relationships, group stages seem to evolve through the three levels of structure: social, interpersonal, and personal.

- Group stages also seem to evolve as a cycle – beginning at the social level, moving on to the interpersonal level, and then to the personal level. Then, from the personal level, groups seem to return to the interpersonal level and often to the social level too.

- These levels are parallel to the elements of the paradox of talk, in that the social level is parallel to the Completing mode, the Interpersonal level is parallel to the Separating mode, and the Personal level is parallel to the Connecting mode.

- Therefore, the full combination cycle seems to include all the communication modes of the paradox of talk.

- Some groups move from one phase to another only by experiencing crises. The dynamics of crises are different from those of phases.

- During phases, stabilising is emphasised and incremental changes are pursued.

- During crises, amplifying is stressed and transformational changes are evident.

- Not all groups need all the phases and all the crises.

- Phases are determined by the purpose of the group.

- Crises erupt only when group members are ambivalent about entering a new phase.

- Clarifying is needed during both phases and crises.

- To benefit from the inclusive stance a binocular view is needed where the full communication cycle of eight stages is seen as a source from which each worker can derive the particular cycle that may best suit each group.

In Part 2 all of these ideas will be demonstrated through the story of working with one group.

Part 2

Applying the
Inclusive Blueprint

'... *all stand in mutuality to a living centre and are in a living relation, a mutual relation, to one another.*'

Martin Buber (1963)

What are the choices available for working with each group?

Part 2 will demonstrate the full range of options as potential stages for all groups. The concepts needed were clarified in Chapter 1, and the rationale for the framework was developed in Chapter 2. Now it is possible to draw on both to help practitioners clarify their choices.

The discussion may be helpful in at least five ways:

- Choosing the stages that may be included while working with each group
- Identifying turning points during each stage
- Anticipating dilemmas that call for sustaining the tension between polarities
- Maintaining flexibility in choosing and constructing group stages
- Ensuring that the choices are all related to one another as various manifestations of the same set of concepts.

As explained at the end of Chapter 2, a binocular view of group stages is needed for this framework. It is necessary to maintain an *overview* of all potential stages. Then a *selected view* of the stages can be developed.

The inclusive blueprint is the common pool of stages: it is a detailed overview of all the stages that may appear in interpersonally oriented time-limited groups. As explained in Part 1, the full range of stages of the inclusive blueprint will appear only when group members are involved in exploring both power and affect (or intimacy), and when members are ambivalent about exploring both issues.

Yet, the binocular view will prevent fragmentation. To use Martin Buber's terms: 'all will stand in mutuality to a living centre ...'. A living centre will be preserved by constructing the stages in terms that are parallel to the paradox of talk. All the ideas will be organised as three-cornered worlds that revolve around that single point: the paradox of talk.

The inclusive blueprint will be articulated in the following four chapters (Chs. 3, 4, 5, 6). Each chapter will include two sections and each section will be dedicated to one stage. All the eight stages will be discussed under the same headings in this order:

The example

First, an example of typical exchanges during that stage will be offered.

Perhaps it may be helpful to comment that the manner of choosing the episodes and analysing them owes much to the pioneering work of Cohen and Smith (1971; 1972). Yet, in this book Cohen and Smith's Critical-Incident approach to leadership interventions is modified to account for a systems view of group relationships.

The eight very brief episodes do not refer to complete stages of group development. Instead, each episode attempts to capture the crucial dynamics of one of the stages of the blueprint. Not only are the examples mere samples of possible scenarios. Each episode has been constructed from working with a number of groups and supervising work with a few more. To save space, each is a condensed version rather than a full-length example.

An important note of caution is needed when such an approach is taken. Because the examples have to be short, they are bound to be somewhat artificial. As a result, the exchanges among members may not be entirely realistic, and workers' responses may appear stereotypical and too perfect. I trust that while you read the scenarios you will be able to enrich these brief conversations by drawing on your own experiences.

The chosen example is of working with a group of parents who have physically harmed their children. The context of working with this group is a British social services office. I chose this context so that various relationships, even those embedded in the use of legal procedures to protect children, are included.

Certain outcomes are anticipated in such a group. The outcomes include reducing the rate and severity of harmful behaviour of these parents towards their children; ideally, to nil. It is also hoped that instead of harming their children, these parents will find satisfactory ways of relating to their children and enable the children's further development. As will be explained, to promote these outcomes the workers accept that the group may have to explore the full range of the inclusive blueprint. The workers also consider it important to encourage the parents to help one another by forming themselves into a network of mutual aid. These workers intend to urge members to consult each other whenever one of them feels the danger of harming his or her child.

Ideally, the dynamics of each family as a whole would have been explored and the parents' involvement in systems outside the group would have been part of the work too. Yet, the examples will not include all these aspects. This partial view is the result of having limited space. The major aim in constructing the example will be only to highlight the main features of the inclusive blueprint.

After each annotated example, the discussion of each stage will be divided into the same sections:

Contents: Group themes and dilemmas

As explained in Chapter 1, contents contain tensions and bring forth the Completing aspect of communication. Contents comprise speech acts, themes and dilemmas. However, the discussion will refer only to the latter two.

This section shows the themes, the emerging dilemmas and the paradox underlying each stage. Not all the possible dilemmas and paradoxes of each stage will be explored, but only ones that can be included within the available space.

Choosing the appropriate level

In Chapter 1, it was explained that the patterns that led to creating structures in groups tended to separate communication into three levels: social, interpersonal, and personal. Now the relevance of these levels to pitching involvement during each stage will be explored.

Processes

In Chapter 2, processes were seen as types of feedback that connect people with one another. Now these types of feedback: amplifying, stabilising, and clarifying will be demonstrated.

Processes are no mysterious phenomena. Some processes stem from the communication among group members, while others are mobilised by the workers. When workers mobilise processes they resort to identifiable skills. Therefore, the comments will be combined with references to groupwork skills that may be employed when facilitating each type of feedback. The purpose of making these references is not to prescribe the particular skills. The aim is merely to demonstrate as concretely as possible how rather well-known groupwork skills may be applied in facilitating major groupwork processes.

Simply to ease the reading, specific references to the sources for each skill will not be made in the texts, but I would like to acknowledge the sources I have used.

There will be ample use of the work of Middleman and Goldberg Wood (1990) when referring to the skills of softening messages, amplifying messages, validating angry feelings, bridging the difference between members and worker, verbalising norms, reaching for a feeling link, reaching for consensus, reaching for difference, re-directing messages, confrontation, challenging blocks, breaking taboos, proposing larger goals, voicing group achievement, and encouraging rituals.

Toseland and Rivas (1984) will be the source for the skills of goal setting, giving advice, suggestion and instruction, re-defining the problem as a group issue, confrontation, resolving conflicts, maintaining and generalising change, and expanding members' social networks.

The writing of Anderson (1984) will underpin references to the skills of contracting, confrontation, challenging blocks, resolving conflicts, reaching for a feeling link, supporting communication in taboo areas, and relating here-and-now to then-and-here.

Corey, Corey, Callanan and Russell (1992) is another source of material about the skills of bridging the difference between members and worker, reaching for difference, breaking taboos, enabling the expression of negative feelings about the group, and eliciting outcomes and plans.

Benson (1987) will be a source for demonstrating the skill of enabling members to own negative feelings.

Further implications for practice

Each chapter will end with further thoughts about three issues:

Turning points

Crucial events that may present workers with important choices between different responses will be identified. The comments will suggest how a practitioner may benefit from the present concepts in choosing her or his response to each of these turning points.

Sustaining polarities

Dilemmas that may arise during this stage will be identified – alerting workers to the need to sustain the tension between their polarities.

Relevance of this stage

The last comment will refer to considerations that may help workers decide whether this stage is relevant to a particular group, and references to examples which can be found in well established groupwork texts will be offered.

A preview of the inclusive blueprint

It may assist you in following the presented explorations by first seeing all the stages by name. In order that you have an overview of the issues to be explored in each chapter, here is a summary again:

Overview of the stages

Stage	Paradox	Process	Level
Forming the group (Ch. 3)	Involvement	Mainly Stabilising and Clarifying, mild Amplifying	Social
Engagement Phase (Ch. 3)	Trust and Reciprocity	Mainly Clarifying and Stabilising, slight Amplifying	Social to Interpersonal
Authority Crisis (Ch. 4)	Authority	Amplifying and Clarifying, weak Stabilising	Abandon Social to re-define Interpersonal
Empowerment Phase (C. 4)	Identity	Mainly Clarifying and Stabilising, no Amplifying	Interpersonal
Intimacy Crisis (Ch. 5)	Intimacy	First Amplifying, Clarifying, later Stabilising	From Inter-personal to Personal
Mutuality Phase (Ch. 5)	Regression and Creativity	Mainly Clarifying, some Amplifying, mild Stabilising	Personal
Separation Crisis (Ch. 6)	Courage	Mainly Amplifying, active Clarifying, little Stabilising	From Personal to Interpersonal
Termination Phase (Ch. 6)	Dependency	Mainly Stabilising, active Clarifying, no Amplifying	Interpersonal and Social

CHAPTER 3

Forming the Group and the Engagement Phase

This chapter will explore the preliminary period of Forming the Group and the Engagement phase.

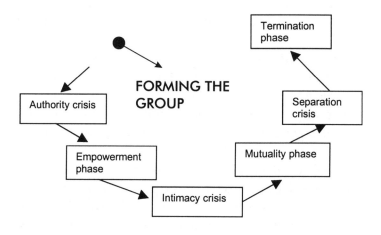

Figure 3.1 Forming the group

Main features of Forming the Group

The paradox of involvement may emerge while forming the group. This stage takes place mostly at the social level. The feedback processes are distinct too: clarifying is paramount, stabilising is considerable, but amplifying is effected only to some extent.

The group starts now, when two social workers: Jane Whiting and Clive Farrow, decide to undertake this time-limited project. Jane is white and Clive is black. This is a deliberate choice as the referrals they receive from their colleagues in the office are racially mixed.

The parents invited to the group have informed their social workers that they want to join a group where they can learn to avoid hurting their children and develop better relationships with them. Both parties agree to focus on members' relationships with their children, and these include discipline and thereby *power issues,* as well as *bonding;* that is, *affective* concerns.

Clive and Jane do not know yet whether the members will be ambivalent about exploring these issues. Yet, these workers do expect the members to feel very ashamed of the harmful consequences of their ways of handling power as well as affect as both issues arise when parents raise their children. The members are also likely to sense that they will have to reveal their feelings in these difficult and possibly embarrassing areas. Therefore, the workers accept that the members may well feel ambivalent about exploring both power and affect.

Put together, these expectations lead Clive and Jane to foresee the advantages of letting the group develop through all the stages of the inclusive blueprint.

The referrals arrive from colleagues in the office, but Clive and Jane take full responsibility for the case management of group members for the duration of the group. These workers are accountable to a team leader and receive groupwork consultation from a specialist in this area of practice (Manor 1989). Eight members are invited after taking care to create a mixed group regarding marital status and racial origin.

Each member or couple is seen by one of the workers before the group begins. In these preliminary interviews the purpose of the group is clarified and prospective members' readiness to join this group is established. Jane and Clive take care to spell out the accountability arrangements within which they work. It is agreed that the group will meet in the social services office for 90 minutes each week for six months.

Following the preparatory interviews (Manor 1988), Jane and Clive convey the agreements with prospective members to the long-term social workers involved with each. Clive and Jane also agree with these social workers as to how they are going to let them know of the progress made by the clients they have referred.

In practice, the details of forming each group may vary considerably. To aid you in forming an inclusive view, the dynamic features of this stage will be discussed.

Let us look at the themes that may underlie work while forming the group.

Contents: Group themes and dilemmas

It is widely recognised that the group begins from the moment workers start to plan it. The process of forming the group determines a great deal of the experiences to come: leadership style, physical resources, support for the workers, or the safety of the group – the seeds for all are planted while forming the group (Brammer, Abrego and Shostrom 1993, pp.238–242; Corey 1995, pp.84–95; Hodge 1977; Hodge 1985; Manor 1986; Manor 1988; Manor 1989).

Over and above these details, it is also possible to see an underlying paradox. The paradox of involvement (Smith and Berg 1987, pp.95–99), or as I prefer to call it; of 'emerging resources', is often a frustrating experience. Practitioners often talk about having to do so much while having so little to show for it. They know that the formed group will offer more resources to clients than individual approaches. Indeed it will do so, but not yet: for now, a great deal of energy has to be invested in the system that will generate these resources.

Planning, formulating their groupwork proposal, receiving referrals, and securing support, consultation, and supervision – all these activities do not involve groupworkers in direct work with clients. These very time consuming activities seem rather remote from actually helping the clients. Yet, planning and organising solidly are very necessary if clients are to benefit from the extra resources generated through participating in the group. The paradox of emerging resources is that in order to offer all clients more, workers need first to give each of them less.

The same is true while meeting clients to prepare them for the group. The temptation is often to deepen the preparatory interview and so fully assess the client and even offer some immediate help. Experienced groupworkers know how to avoid this trap. They remember that if they deepen their involvement with each client, the chances are that these clients will develop expectations of them as 'their' workers. Later on, when these clients join the group they may well be less motivated to invest energy in being involved with their peers. So, by giving members so much so early, workers may actually deprive clients of receiving what they cannot give: mutual support and a continuous source of help from their peers. Mutual aid among group members is an example of an emergent resource. In order to offer clients more opportunities to generate this resource, workers need at first to be less personally involved with them. As Smith and Berg (1987, p.99) put it: 'the ability to be involved is tied to the ability to be removed'. Instead of a deeply personal session, the preparatory interview should be focused on the processes involved in the client joining the group.

Choosing the appropriate level: The social level

The previous discussion suggests that 'forming the group tests the workers' brokering abilities. Workers have to spend time on many social activities. They have to negotiate resources as well as clarify and sometimes remove constraints. They also have to create links with other professionals who control referrals and financial resources, supervisors and consultants.

As these processes are mobilised, a structure begins to emerge. While forming the group, workers are, so to speak, carving a niche for it within an existing web of other social systems. Workers are able to do so because they are 'workers' – they are sanctioned by an agency to form this group. At first, most of the workers' activities are conducted from that position. Workers approach referral sources as 'groupworkers', and referrers respond as 'social workers', or in other situations – as 'teachers', or as 'doctors', or as 'policemen'. It is well to remember that referral sources have their own concerns: teachers are worried about education, doctors are alert to issues of health, and so on. Referrers react within the social definitions of their own disciplines. At the stage of making a referral these professionals apply their judgement beyond the differences that mark groupworkers as individuals. Therefore, groupworkers may want to focus on the social level: addressing potential referrers in terms that are current within the referrers' own professional worlds. Understanding this may help workers talk with referral sources in ways that enlist their co-operation (Manor 1984, pp.48–53). Such collaboration is first formed at the social level that permeates inter-disciplinary practices.

Likewise, while meeting the prospective group members, groupworkers are well advised to bear the social level in mind. It is best that potential members see them first and foremost as representatives of the agency who suggest a *different* form of help. If these clients do not see the workers in this way, they are likely to turn them into their new individual workers. This is an image groupworkers may wish to avoid. Groupworkers can escape this pitfall by focusing the preparatory interview on the relevance of the proposed group to each member, rather than deepening involvement to the level of that client's intimate personal concerns. By doing this, the groupworkers clarify the relevance of the emerging group and the potential of other group members as a source of help that no worker can provide (Manor 1986; Manor 1988).

So, this interview will have a personal touch; some experiences will be expressed by each member as an individual who is different from other individuals. Yet, personal references will be restricted. For example, the emphasis may be on personal experiences related to the member's social role of being parents, but not go beyond these to explore marital relationships. From a systems point of view, parental concerns are mainly interpersonal – charging the social roles of being parents with personal meaning.

Altogether, a competent way of conducting the preparatory interview probably involves focusing on social concerns combined with relevant interpersonal references, while avoiding too many personal revelations.

> *Forming the Group is focused at the Social level with only relevant Interpersonal references, and relatively few personal exchanges being encouraged.*

Processes

Processes tend to emphasise Connecting experiences with one another, and three major feedback processes are discussed here.

Clarifying

Clarifying is creating a link among experiences that charges them with new meaning.

Planning the group, formulating a groupwork proposal, receiving referrals, preparing potential members, and securing support, consultation, and supervision all raise similar concerns. How will the workers ensure that their methods meet clients' needs? How will they liaise with referrers? Will the workers' superiors understand the requirements of this particular group? To answer such questions it is necessary to make links and offer new ones, among perceptions held by people in all the sub-systems. Answering these questions, the workers create connections among the clients' systems, their own systems as groupworkers, and that of the agency. Inevitably, workers charge these relationships with new meaning. In systems terms, Clarifying is paramount during these activities.

Stabilising

Stabilising is steering interactions towards a pre-determined range.

While the workers are busy clarifying the plan for the group, they also aim to form a sufficiently well-defined system: the group. Workers know that this system is going to change from the moment its members meet, but each group does need a launch pad – an identifiable starting point. This is why, at this stage, groupworkers have to take a gamble. Workers know that the initial arrangement will be altered by group members later on, but they have to begin with the option that makes most sense to them.

To set the group wheels in motion, the workers have to choose a viable framework. In our example, the workers opt for a closed group of eight adults meeting for 90 minutes every week for six months. The rest of the workers' activities are guided by the need to lead all the sub-systems towards this initial option first. A certain arrangement has to be on the workers' minds, and their efforts have to be directed towards achieving it in a planned step-by-step fashion. In systems terms, the workers will be effecting a great deal of Stabilising.

Amplifying

Amplifying is continuously intensifying a deviation from an established range of interactions.

By seeking referrals and by meeting the potential members to prepare them for the group, the workers also deliver to clients an unpalatable message: 'you need more than other members of the public; there is a sense in which you are different and that's why we are here'. There is no way of denying the fact that only potential clients are approached by professionals with an offer of help, while others are not. Even if the workers call clients 'users', the latter's need for help is implicit. So, the workers' involvement, no matter how it is phrased, is likely to intensify clients' awareness of being less self-sufficient than other members of the public. Whether workers intend it or not, the result of their approach to clients is that this 'deviation', or disturbing experience, of needing professional help, is more acutely experienced. In systems terms, Amplifying is effected to some extent.

> *While Forming the Group Clarifying is paramount, Stabilising is considerable, and Amplifying is effected to some extent too.*

Further implications for practice

Forming the group is not always considered a stage of group development. Perhaps this is one of the reasons why some groups do not engage sufficiently and why many lose members who said they would want to come. Here is where understanding systems can help a great deal. The people who may join the group do not live in a vacuum, but with other systems such as families, neighbours, landlords, employers and many more. Each potential member also has memories of groups to which she or he has belonged. Inviting a person to join a new group perturbs the systems with which this person is already involved: present ones, as well as ones evoked by memories of past groups. This is probably why joining a new group can sometimes be a rather daunting prospect for the members.

It is true that not every group raises the same worries for prospective members. The worker who thinks with systems in mind can anticipate this difference. If the intended group is for people who already know one another; that is, they are already a loosely formed system, then each member is less likely to be worried about joining that new group. This may be the case in forming a new group from among the clients of a day centre, as these clients already know each other. Yet, forming a new group from referrals of parents by a health visitor is a very different matter. These parents do not know one another, and so – they are likely to be more worried about the nature of the new group, and the reactions in other systems that form their environment.

The second aspect arises out of the purpose of the group. A group designed to enable members to explore the effects of being sexually abused is clearly different from one that aims to educate them about safe sex. In both groups, sex will be mentioned, but in the group for sexually-abused young women the experiences are likely to be far more personal than in the sex education group. The level at which the group is expected to work will be different. The more personal the intended explorations, the more care should be taken to prepare members for the experience of the group.

If the group is expected to explore personal issues then it is better that recruitment and preparation are by face to face interaction and cover all the issues included in the stage of Forming the Group.

Summary

Forming the Group gives rise to the paradox of involvement (or 'emerging resources'). Handling this paradox involves a great deal of clarifying. Stabilising is paramount, and amplifying disturbing experiences occurs to some extent too. These processes are best steered towards the social level. Some interpersonal references are relevant, but many personal ones are very rarely appropriate.

One way or another, Forming the Group is always a relevant stage. Strategies adopted while forming the group influence a great deal of what is to come. The accounts of failures in groupwork often reveal problems related to neglecting or mishandling aspects of this stage. Indeed, when a systems view is adopted, setting up a new group cannot but be seen as the first stage of creating a new system, and therefore, a stage that needs the workers' full attention.

Now it is possible to see how the group meets for the first time.

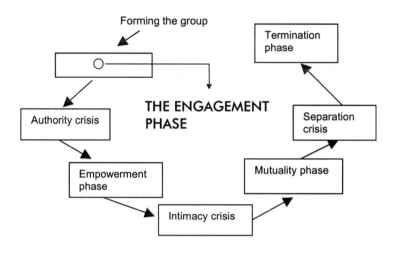

Figure 3.2 The Engagement phase

Main features of this stage

The Engagement phase gives rise to the paradox of trust: to encourage members to trust them, the workers have to convey trust in the members first. The first session involves the social level, and thereafter relationships shift to the interpersonal one.

During the Engagement phase Clarifying is paramount, stabilising is considerable and Amplifying is slight.

The example

It is 7.30pm. The workers are already in the room and have arranged enough chairs in a circle. The members begin to arrive: some in pairs and others on their own. Each worker welcomes the members he or she knows; inviting them to make themselves comfortable and sit down where they want. When all are in the room the workers sit down too; each opposite the other.

The group members are:

> Betty Carr; of African-Caribbean culture, concerned about her relationship with her daughter Sammy.

> Joyce and John Cook; of white culture, concerned about their relationship with their daughter Ruth.

> Assiff Khan (married); of Indian culture, concerned about his relationship with his daughter Jasmin.

Moira Morris; of white origin, concerned about her relationship with her daughter Kathy.

Jean and Gerald Robinson; of African-Caribbean origin, concerned about their relationship with their son Jimmy.

David Thomas; of white origin, concerned about his relationship with his son Mike.

Two groupworkers work with this group:

Clive Farrow of African-Caribbean origin.

Jane Whiting of white origin.

For the sake of brevity they will be called 'workers'.

Please, note: references to the *Child Protection Register* will be made in this example. This register documents every family whose children are at risk of being harmed, as required of social workers by British law. The terms 'groupworker', 'worker', and 'practitioner' will be used to mean the same position: a person who offers groupwork to clients or users.

After a brief introduction, the workers set the process in motion:

1. Clive: So, to start with, some people know you, Jane, but not me, and the other way round, of course. Also, many don't know one another. Let's get to know one another first. I know we'll probably be talking about quite difficult things, but I hope we'll also help one another and have some good times (smiles). It's not against the law, is it, I mean having good time? Let's see. Let's go round – say our names and one good thing, yeah – fun thing, that happened to us recently. As I said, I'm Clive Farrow. A good thing that happened to me recently was that an old friend came to visit from abroad. I really enjoyed our time together. How about everybody else?

2. David Thomas: What, me?

3. Jane: That'll be nice.

4. David Thomas: Well, I suppose. I am David Thomas. Ah, one good thing. I don't know. Well, my mum came over on Sunday. The thing is; this time we did not argue.

5. Clive: It was good not to argue for a change.

6. John Cook: I'm John Cook. One good thing: last Sunday I did not cook. Joyce did (laughter all round).

(conversations continue in this manner until everybody is introduced)

7. Clive: It's good to hear about the good things. As you know, Jane met some of you and I met others to talk about this group, because social workers had been concerned about what had been happening with your children. Obviously, each of you is worried too. That's why we are here. We thought that it might help getting together. Perhaps together each of us can find ways of getting over the difficulties, so you don't have to worry so much, and yes – you may have even more good times with the kids.

8. Jean Robinson: But we do have good time!

9. Jane: You do, and at the same time there are worries. Let's see. I wonder if we feel comfortable enough now: what would each of you want to be different when this group ends? I wonder. Can we hear examples?

10. Joyce Cook: Well… (long silence)

11. Jean Robinson: How do you mean 'different'?

12. Clive: Better?

13. Betty Carr: Well, I'd certainly appreciate fewer sleepless nights.

14. Gerald Robinson: If anybody knows how to get him to come in on time…

15. Jane: Him?

16. Gerald Robinson: Well, Jimmy our son. He WILL have to be in on time.

17. Clive: Gerald, are you saying that you want to find other ways of making sure Jimmy is safe?

18. Jean Robinson: Well …

19. Assiff Khan: (quietly and slowly) Boys these days …

20. Clive: Is it finding out how else to get on with them, Assiff?

21. Assiff Khan: Well, you are the professionals.

22. Jane: Any hope you have, Moira?

23. Moira Morris: Hope! I'm a bit old for that, don't you think?

24. Jane: Sounds like it's been tough for you, Moira.

25. Moira Morris: Well, I think I'll pass on that one if it's all right with you.

26. Jane: You'd rather wait with talking about this. (Moira Morris stares at the floor).

27. Clive: I appreciate you saying it so straight, Moira. For me, in this group, the main thing is if we could be straight with each other.

28. Jane: People have good reasons for taking their time, and I hope we'll learn to hear and respect this.

(conversation continues until all members who want to do so give examples)

29. Jane: You may not believe this, but I think we are already getting on with it. We certainly have good examples now.

How then? How will we get there? What can each of us do which may help? Clive and I shall be here every week. We can help, for example by helping everyone speak. Sometimes it's difficult to find our way in a group. Perhaps we can also help people to listen. Because of our training, sometimes we may see some things, which are happening while those of you involved with the kids will not. It's like seeing the wood for the trees, you know. Because the reality is that we are not in it ourselves, perhaps we can ...

30. Moira Morris: You are not in it, are you?

31. Clive: You sound a bit angry, Moira.

32. Moira Morris: I'm not angry. I'm straight.

33. Jane: Yes, you are, and another thing which will help is if everybody else is straight too. Also, sometimes it's a matter of making ourselves clear, isn't it?

34. Moira Morris (tensely): Well, one thing IS clear.

35. Clive: One thing?

36. Moira Morris: There is one register, that's clear.

37. Jane: You mean Moira, that being put on the At Risk Register, and being taken off is not clear?

38. David Thomas: Well, let's face it. You have the power.

39. Clive: Ah, I think I'm getting it.

40. Jane: Is it about the criteria? Who will decide about putting your names on the Child Protection Register and how will they decide?

41. David Thomas: Well, I for one would like to know.

42. Clive: I'd be surprised David, if you are the only one. (looking around the room, members are nodding with approval) It's good that we talk about it now.

43. Jane: There's often a lot of confusion about it, for us too. As far as I understand it the thinking is actually quite simple. It's that thing called 'the safety of a child'. If there is any reason to worry about any of your children being at risk of being hit, or being neglected or that their health suffers, or being treated so they are too upset to be helped inside the family, then we shall have to do something. I think that's it.

44. David Thomas: What? Are you saying that we don't love our children enough to do something ourselves?

45. Clive: That is perhaps the most difficult thing. Both Jane and I talked about each of you after we'd met with each. We know you love your children. We really do. (attentive silence in the room)

46. Jane: That's exactly why we must talk about it all. You do love each of your children. Yet, something's gone wrong. You know this. You know you love, and in spite of it …

47. Clive: That's the difficult bit isn't it; (pauses) loving them, and then it somehow gets out of hand and they're hurt. You hurt too, we know this. So, we must find other ways …

48. Betty Carr: But there's a bottom line.

49. Clive: Well, there is. We'll just confuse each other if we ignore it.

50. Betty Carr: At least you are straight.

(long and uneasy silence)

51. Joyce Cook: Well, it IS your job.

(more long silence)

52. Jean Robinson: To be honest, I can't say I LIKE it.

53. David Thomas: I don't really, but then … At least it's all above board …

54. Gerald Robinson: I suppose. It's knowing what's what.

55. Jane: I'd like to hear from more members how each feels about all these issues.

(processing continues until contracting is possible)

56. Clive: What will help with all this is each of you raising any worry you have without waiting to be asked. I know it takes some practice, but that's how each of you can help. Also, listening to one another, comparing notes about handling similar situations with the kids. There is no one way, but the more examples we hear the better.

57. Jane: Sometimes it may help doing exercises about reacting to different people and to the kids. Sometimes we may even want to watch some films about this. It may help.

These are our ideas, but we hope you will also suggest how best to help each other. After all, you know; you are in it. (Gerald Robinson looks at his watch)

58. Clive: Jane, I think some people are concerned about the time.

59. Moira Morris: Yes, what times shall we meet?

(practicalities about the day and time of sessions are discussed until agreement is reached)

60. Jane: OK then, see you next Tuesday 7.30 here.

This is where the exchanges end. As you have noticed, because space is limited the example does not go beyond the first session. Since the first session sets the tone for so much that is to come, it seemed necessary to settle for demonstrating its dynamics on their own. Now it is time see the picture as a whole. The first step is to see how the containing contents may be separated into themes.

Contents: Group themes and dilemmas

As explained in Chapter 2, during the Engagement phase members try to form a complete picture of the emerging group.

This is probably why the first session is likely to have a marked effect on the future development of the group. During the first session, practitioners often concentrate on building the working alliance (Pinsof 1994). They set the tone and atmosphere, achieve some shared understanding of the purpose of the group, and clarify the ways and means of pursuing the agreed purposes.

Fostering the working alliance; between the workers and the members, as well as among the members themselves, often needs special attention. The reason is not difficult to find: to each member the others are strangers at first. Others are simply members of the public who will now know of the person's difficulties by virtue of being members of the same group. Each member fears that others may pass judgement, they may even pass on gossip. Is it worth it? Can the members be trusted to be helpful? Each member has to find out whether the others are trustworthy and whether it is possible to form a working alliance with them. One source of trust that members expect to be already available is the workers.

Workers who understand all this can do a great deal to alleviate these valid fears. Workers who start from members' strengths can show members right from the start that they trust members' inner resources and innate capabilities to get over the problems. Conveying such optimistic messages can foster members' hope. Such a message may indicate that further positive experiences may arise out of their membership in this group instead of the negative judgement they dread. This is why the workers begin the session with a growth game about members' constructive experiences (entries 1–6).

Pinsof (1994) also highlighted the value of *agreeing on achievable goals* right from the start. Members' willingness to trust the workers is usually enhanced when members realise the purpose of taking the risk of talking to strangers. This is why the workers focus on members' goals so early in the session. You can see this intention behind Jane's question, when she asks (entry 9): 'What would each of you want to be different when this group ends?'

Yet, more work is needed to further members' trust even after goals are clarified. Trust has to be gained rather than claimed. The workers have to demonstrate to members reasons why the members can trust them with regard to various issues. This is why the workers' reactions to Moira Morris, who refuses to indicate her goals, are so important. Notice that neither Jane nor Clive pressurises Moira Morris to state her goals. Instead, Jane communicates empathy to Moira's refusal (entry 26), and Clive uses the opportunity to clarify that '… the main thing is if we could be straight with each other' (entry 27). Both workers convey trust in the members' judgement. As Jane says: 'People have good reasons for taking their time' (entry 28).

Trusting the members' judgement is conveyed also by the workers' willingness to provide members with all the information they possess about the organisation of the group. Offering such full explanations is a way of saying to members that they are trusted to make good judgement once they know what is going on.

Such explanations also address the third component of the working alliance (Pinsof 1994): *the tasks*; that is, what could help achieving the goals. So, the workers describe what they intend to do in the group and how they plan to go about it. The workers very openly respond to the hints members offer about the power difference between them. When Moira Morris says to the workers: 'You are not in it, are you?' (entry 30), the workers let her say a little more rather than ignore the message as an aside. The dialogue leads Moira (entry 34) and then David Thomas (entry 38) to raise an important question: the powers workers possess to notify their superiors of concerns about the safety of any child involved; that is, to put members' names on the Child Protection Register. This important issue is then fully clarified.

In parallel, the workers also suggest what members themselves can do to make the experience helpful. These suggestions are offered right from the start. Indeed, already in entry 7, you can see Clive acknowledging the existence of problems, and even saying: 'That's why we are here'. Yet, Clive does not drown the discussion with worries. Instead, he immediately works towards identifying shared tasks. By talking about 'getting together' as a way of 'getting over the difficulties', he focuses members' minds on that which may help. More suggestions are put forward in entries 33, 56, and 57.

This session ends by reaching agreement about the practicalities of meeting together (entries 81–89); often called 'contracting'.

One of the dilemmas that arise at this stage revolves around trust. The paradox of trust (Smith and Berg 1987, pp.115–120) seems to underscore the workers' attitudes: for members to trust the workers these workers have first to show that they trust the members.

Workers who appreciate this paradox may not wait until they know they can fully trust the members. Mindful of the paradox involved, such workers will find those aspects with which they can already trust the members as the group begins, and then acknowledge these aspects very explicitly. Taking the initiative in conveying trust may generate more trust in the group as a whole.

Trust is of value not only for launching the group. In itself, increased trust may be beneficial to members as it may contribute towards furthering some of the curative factors identified by Yalom (1995, pp.69–105). As yet, there is not enough knowledge to prescribe these benefits for each stage, but practice experience would suggest that increased trust may contribute to members' experience of group cohesiveness; as in 'Feeling alone no longer' and to interpersonal learning as output; for example, 'Feeling more trustful of groups and of other people'.

So much for the dilemmas included in these contents. In your own practice you may not hold such legal powers, and anyhow there may be other differences which may lead to further dilemmas. Yet, the essential processes and levels may be rather similar, and these will be explored now.

Choosing the appropriate level: Between the social and the interpersonal

The optimal level of group involvement is one that enables members to articulate dilemmas in which members are involved.

You can see that in this example, the workers first pitch their involvement mainly at the social level. Important workers' interventions are addressed to the group as a whole: the initial recognition of the problem (entries 7, 45–47), the explanations of workers' powers (entry 43), the advice about constructive participation (entries 56, 57) – all these are matters that concern the members beyond the differences among them. These are social concerns that stem from their roles as members and the workers' roles as workers.

Of course, interpersonal experiences are elicited too. The fun game that Clive initiates in entry 1, invites each member to express her or his version of events; and thus, members who participate in the game are bound to convey individual perceptions that mark each as different. Yet, these excursions into personal matters are light hearted, and do not as yet touch upon the painful issues that have brought the members to the group. When members' difficulties are approached by Jane (entry 9), they are turned round – into goals that members may identify for themselves. By their nature, such self-identified goals have to be personalised, but at this stage, the goals will probably identify outcomes that relate to members in the roles of parents. The goals will be their own versions of taking the role of parents more satisfactorily. So, the goals are likely to be formulated at the interpersonal level where each member charges the social role of being a parent with personal meaning derived from being different from other parents.

The relevance of a group's pattern to the level of group interaction was already suggested in Chapter 1. When a group is initially grounded so firmly in the social level as in this example, the group will tend to evolve its relationships around the pattern known as the wheel. Within the pattern of the wheel, the workers occupy a central position and the members relate in a parallel fashion to the workers more than to each other. Within the structure of the wheel members are relatively separate from one another. This pattern has its advantages in restricting personal expressions among members and thus decreasing the risk of as yet unmanageable experiences from surfacing.

Altogether, the Engagement phase begins at the Social level and gradually shifts to the Interpersonal one.

Processes

Clarifying

The paradox of trust directs the workers to concentrate on making the experiences of joining the group as meaningful to the members as possible. To do this, the workers try to create, suggest, and point out as many links among the bewildering experiences as they can. This means that clarifying is paramount during the first session.

You can see the workers responding with empathy quite often; for example when Gerald Robinson states that Jimmy, his son, 'will have to be in on time' (entry 16), Clive responds to the underlying message, of caring for the boy, by saying: 'Gerald, are you saying that you want to find other ways of making sure Jimmy is safe?' (entry 17). Other examples of empathy can be seen in entries 20, 24, 26, 31, and 37.

Drawing out more specific messages from members is also a way of clarifying communication. You can see how Jane draws out from Gerald Robinson a more specific reference to his son (entry 15), and how Clive enables Jean Robinson to focus on aiming for future situations to be 'better' rather than just different, in entry 12.

Yet, these workers are not only client-centred. At this stage, they appreciate that providing guidance and explanations can enhance trust, and so you can see Jane reflecting approvingly on the value of people 'taking their time' (entry 28); particularly later, when she spells out what she and Clive may be able to do to be helpful to the group (entry 29). The workers go even further in this direction by pointing out what members themselves may do to help the process along (entries 33, and particularly 56, 57). This very explicit form of guidance is not always provided, but the present workers, mindful of how Clarifying may contribute to trust, choose to offer a great deal of this feedback.

As you reflect upon these observations, you are likely to realise that many of the workers' responses are combinations of Clarifying and Stabilising. Indeed, apart from some purely behavioural methods, Stabilising is usually offered with a Clarifying component attached to it, to render the messages meaningful. Still, some responses emphasise Stabilising very clearly.

Stabilising

Clive's first intervention (entry 1), of asking about good things that happened to members, is a form of growth game (Manor and Dumbleton, 1993). Yet, in this example, Clive draws on this game as a form of Stabilising. Parents who join a group like the present one, often feel they have failed their children. As a result, their self-esteem is rather low. Many of the workers' initial interventions may well aim to counteract group members' low morale; which is a form of stabilising. Indeed, in the example, Clive uses this game to counteract members' feelings of being viewed as failures. In entry 5, when Clive says to David Thomas: 'It was good not to argue for a change', Clive implicitly recognises David's ability to handle a situation well. Many of the workers' other interventions are aimed at shifting members' preoccupation away from failure and towards achievable goals. Indeed, goal setting by Clive can be seen in entry 7, and Jane elicits such goals from the members in entry 9.

Drawing on their appreciation of the paradox of trust, the workers provide guidance and advice to members; conveying the message that they trust the members to make good use of the information. The workers offer members guidance about specific contributions that members can make to help the work; for example, 'be straight with each other' (entries 27 and 33), 'listening to one another, comparing notes' (entry 56), and participating in exercises (entry 57). Such direct suggestions imply that there is a desirable range of behaviours towards which group members are steered by the workers. Offering such directive suggestions is, of course, a form of Stabilising.

Verbalising norms (entries 43, 49) contributes to the same Stabilising effect, and voicing group achievements by praising members for 'getting on with it' (entry 29) is an explicit way of Stabilising interactions towards the desired range.

Amplifying

When meeting the group for the first time it is often tempting to enhance the deepening of self-revelations by members. Yet, groupworkers who appreciate members' dilemmas during the Engagement phase do not fall for this hastily. Such workers appreciate that a working alliance based on trust has to be established first. Therefore, Amplifying disturbing experiences is very minimal during this phase. Still, some reference to members' problems is necessary. You can see Clive restricting himself to saying: 'I know we'll probably be talking about quite difficult things' in entry 1, and then quickly moving away to 'good things' first.

As mentioned before, members of such a group already experience themselves as different from other members of the public: as having encountered problems in being parents. In this sense members see themselves as deviating from expected norms. Yet, the only time this deviation is briefly explored is during entries 45 to 47, when the workers acknowledge that the members are caught in a bind: they both love their children and hurt them at the same time: 'something's gone wrong'…'it somehow gets out of hand'. No more and no less – the reference is explicit yet brief. Amplifying the members' distress does not extend beyond merely identifying it.

During the Engagement phase Clarifying is paramount, Stabilising is considerable, and Amplifying is slight.

Further implications for practice: Turning points, polarities, and relevance of this stage

The manner of writing about each stage may inevitably convey a prescriptive stance that is not intended. This is why I would like to identify choices open to each groupworker who engages a group. The choices are at least of three types: turning points, sustaining polarities, and the relevance of the stage to the particular group.

Turning points

Very few relationships are prescribed recipes, and group relations are no exception. At some points involvement can change course, and groupworkers can be aware of these moments when responding to members. In the example, the first turning point is probably in entry 8, when Jean Robinson protests that members do have good times with their children. The workers could have probed further into this statement, demonstrating that not all the present members always have good times with their children. Yet, the workers do not choose to do this. Instead, Jane (entry 9) directs the group towards identifying interpersonal goals.

Why is this choice? Had Jane encouraged the deepening of Jean Robinson's message, the members might have become involved in more personal concerns. This, Jane and Clive judge to have been premature. The workers' awareness of the optimal level of group involvement for *this* stage, leads them to direct the members to interpersonal concerns that arise as members formulate their own goals.

Another potential turning point occurs when Moira Morris refuses to identify her own hopes (entries 23–25). Again, the workers could have chosen to explore Moira's refusal further. Had they done so, the workers would have abandoned the focus on the interpersonal level, possibly encouraging Moira Morris to express far more personal concerns underlying her refusal. You can see that these workers (entries 26–28) do not encourage such a level of disclosure. The reasons are the same: too personal revelations too early may have not been properly supported by the rest of the group, and so would have left Moira even lonelier than before.

Of course, in other groups the workers may judge the issues to be less demanding and the members to be more ready to support one another even during the first phase of engagement. If so, workers may consciously alter the chosen level for a while. Still, the importance of the interpersonal level may well guide most groupworkers during the Engagement phase.

Sustaining polarities

Realising that at a deeper level all relationships are grounded in a paradox may help groupworkers respond and facilitate the Engagement phase. It was already noted that being aware of the paradox of trust, groupworkers may not hesitate to take the initiative and communicate their trust in the members quite explicitly, rather early on.

In addition, it may be helpful to keep in mind the inevitable tension between Stabilising and Amplifying. The tendency to amplify members' messages and thereby elicit the depth of their concerns, is understandable. Yet, the inevitable tie that Amplifying has with stabilising may well remind the groupworkers that Amplifying on its own is not necessarily helpful. To facilitate constructive learning, Amplifying is better tied in with Stabilising. In simpler terms: when considering Amplifying members' disturbing experiences, groupworkers may well sense first whether the members are ready to resort to enough Stabilising; supporting and enabling each other in finding a new level of handling the issue explored. When there is not enough supportive Stabilising in the group, then perhaps it is better to wait a little longer before pursuing the challenge of Amplifying.

Relevance of the Engagement phase

All time-limited groups have to begin at some point, and so are very likely to need an Engagement phase. Yet, the length of this phase may vary considerably.

As mentioned already, the pattern of the Engagement phase will tend to revolve around that of the wheel; with the workers occupying a central position and the members relating in parallel lines to the workers. The advantage of this pattern is in protecting members from too much personal disclosure. Indeed, some groups may benefit from adopting this pattern for most of their time together.

An example of a group that spends most of its time in the Engagement phase can be seen in the account offered by O'Hara (1988). This is a group designed to prepare adults for the tasks of fostering. The aims of the group are educational and so a clear programme is designed in advance. Most readers who will turn to this source will be able to see that all the six sessions offered are led by the workers and revolve around social and interpersonal concerns that intending foster parents have to bear in mind.

Yet, this is not always the case. As the work of Rose and Edleson (1987) shows, after a while, groups for offending adolescents may need to move on from the initial stage. The initial stage which Rose and Edleson (1987, pp.22–27) call 'the orientation phase' focuses on social and interpersonal concerns while the workers resort to many explanations as well as directive interventions that stabilise the group. In this sense Rose and Edleson's (1987) orientation phase is quite similar to the present Engagement phase. Yet, later on Rose and Edleson's model moves to a different dynamic, which they call 'assessment'.

The Engagement phase is needed not only in the relatively structured groups such as the ones described by Rose and Edleson (1987). Even in groups that rely on a very loose structure, the initial stage resembles the present Engagement phase. This can be seen in the work of Benson (1987), who presents a model of groups for personal growth, although he calls this 'the inclusion stage' (Benson 1987, pp.84–102). Such very personal groups certainly do not remain at the Engagement phase for too long, but even these groups do need to pay attention to social and interpersonal concerns first.

As will be seen, while the Engagement phase is needed by all groups, other stages may not be always so clearly pertinent. One of these is the *authority crisis* to which discussion will now turn.

CHAPTER 4

Authority Crisis and the Empowerment Phase

Two stages will be demonstrated in this chapter: the Authority crisis and the Empowerment phase.

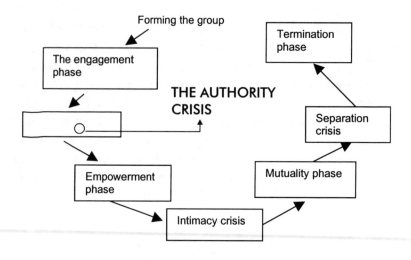

Figure 4.1 The Authority crisis

Main features of this stage

This crisis reveals the paradox of authority: to gain more power you have to empower others. During this crisis the group transforms its boundaries: abandoning the social level, and re-defining the interpersonal one. Amplifying is paramount, clarifying is very actively employed, and stabilising is rather sparsely used.

The example

A few weeks have passed since the first session. This evening, as usual, one of the workers begins the session asking whether anybody has any particular issues they want to raise. Yet, unlike the previous sessions, Jane is met with heavy silence: members are sitting in withdrawn positions, arms folded, and eye contact avoided. About three minutes pass.

1. Joyce Cook: Yes, well…

2. Jean Robinson: Well what?

3. John Cook: Nothing really. Joyce is just … (nodding in disapproval)

4. David Thomas: Wasn't it something? I mean, did you see it last night? What a way to talk!

5. Joyce Cook: Well …

6. David Thomas: That reporter. I bet he had never looked after a single child. For crying out loud! (his voice sinks in despair)

7. Clive: That reporter seemed to have said something, well … painful.

8. Moira Morris: (to male worker in a sharp voice) Painful? Silly I'd call it. (turns abruptly to David Thomas and speaks warmly) You know, it's their job. They don't really mean it.

9. Joyce Cook: Well, I must say, he was a bit over the top.

10. Jane: It's one thing to talk about being a parent and quite another to … (interrupted)

11. Betty Carr: Be one.

12. Moira Morris: People talk, but when it comes to the walk …

13. Clive: I sort of find myself wondering. This must be difficult. We're talking in such general terms; about 'people', about 'reporters', who else?

14. John Cook: (in a cold withdrawn voice) We are all people, you know.

15. Jane: Something about us as people is difficult too?

16. Joyce Cook: (in an apologetic voice) Well, I felt, last week …

17. Jean Robinson: (eagerly) Yeah, what about last week?

18. John Cook: (hurriedly) Well, some weeks are better than others, aren't they?

19. Betty Carr: (in a flat angry voice) Better or worse, I don't mind. It wasn't right.

20. Clive: Something wasn't right last week. We can talk about it, too.

21. Betty Carr: Not something dear, someone!

(silence for about a minute)

22. John Cook: Well, I believe in calling a spade a spade.

23. Clive: Hard as it is, better than sitting around like lemons.

24. Betty Carr: (to male worker) Give us a break Clive, I really think we have had enough theories for one night!

25. Joyce Cook: It's not easy to sit here listening to all this talk about other parents, how perfect THEY are, is it?

26. Jane: Something was difficult last time, but we'd better talk about it.

27. John Cook: Well, to be honest, it was a bit much. (to male worker) It's OK for you to talk, but let's face it, you've never had a child!

28. Clive: I've never had a child of my own.

29. Moira Morris: You talk as if you have.

30. David Thomas: It's a matter of respect, isn't it? You just sit there. You don't get up at night with a screaming kid into your dreams, do you?

31. Jane: Some of us seem to have been hurt by Clive, is that it?

32. Moira Morris: (to female worker) Wouldn't you be?

33. David Thomas: It's a question of respect. But really you don't, do you? You just sit there thinking who will stay on the Register, for how long.

34. Clive: Yes, this is quite painful, but we've got to get through this. True, I do sit here, so does Jane, and yes we do have to think about the Register. You know this. We've agreed on this from the start. I thought it was clear enough, but it isn't. You see, criticising us has nothing to do with your children being at risk. So, it has nothing

to do with being kept on the Register either. Something else must have come up now, on top of the Register.

35. Joyce Cook: It's like you've got the answers. All the answers.

36. Gerald Robinson: I know we've done wrong, but there's no need to rub it in, is there?

37. Jean Robinson: Last week I felt like a kid myself, being told off for being naughty. But I'm no kid by any stretch of the imagination, am I?

38. Clive: I don't see any of you as children, yet I seem to have hurt you. I'll have to find out how. Does anybody remember an example?

39. David Thomas: All that talk Clive, about ignoring the kid being naughty, hugging him when he's good; fine talk. But you never think how hard it is, how he gets on my nerves. You don't respect OUR judgement!

40. Jane: So, it wasn't WHAT Clive said, but THE WAY he said it, was it?

41. Joyce Cook: It was as if we were ignorant.

42. John Cook: As if we couldn't make any judgement at all.

43. Jane: I just wonder, was it just Clive? Both of us have been telling you what to do?

44. Moira Morris: Well since you mention it ...

45. Clive: So what annoyed you was Jane and I coming across as patronising?

46. Betty Carr: That sums it up. Patronising.

47. Jane: Well may be, and if so it's a pity. (pauses) It is true I can't really tell each of you how to handle each and every situation with each of your kids. Knowing Clive, I don't think he sees himself able either.

48. Clive: Certainly not.

49. Gerald Robinson: So: why patronising?

50. Clive: Yes, this makes sense, but you see – I know I can come across like that particularly when others keep asking for advice, or don't say much. I get worried, so I just fill the gap.

51. Joyce Cook: Well, come on, this IS true; we've been leaving a lot to them two, haven't we?

52. Jane: Groups often begin like that, and then find they have to change.

53. Moira Morris: It'll have to change.

54. Clive: We can begin right now. What would help? What could each of us do differently so we work better as a group?

55. Betty Carr: To start with, I don't like being asked if I have a problem at the beginning. If I do, I'll let you know anyhow. I'm not a kid.

56. Jane: So one thing we can change is the way the session begins. Any suggestion?

57. David Thomas: Well, one of us can start. (to Betty Carr) How about you Betty? Why don't you just start the next meeting going round the room. Not asking questions, just checking how people are?

58. Betty Carr: Well, I don't know, if people want me ...

59. John Cook: Come on Betty, you'll be a super-duper worker. No, seriously, it'll be better. I suppose we can take turns?

With this example in mind, let us see themes and dilemmas that connect the contents.

Contents: Group themes and dilemmas

The more ambivalent group members are about the use of power and the less structured the group, the more workers are in for a shock. As the group's life gets 'better', it suddenly turns 'worse'. Often, and without any clear warning, the members appear to gang up on their workers. They criticise their workers for not caring enough; they claim their workers do not know their job; they accuse them of misleading and patronising. This crisis appears to be similar to Tuckman and Jensen's (1977) stage of 'storming'.

As is often the case, quite a number of themes may be emerging in such a group at the same time. Elsewhere (Manor 1997) I have offered a more detailed account of the Authority crisis. Here the focus will be on the experience that contains these aspects: the paradox involved.

The contents in the example revolve around the workers being seen by the members as 'patronising'. Yet, such contents are sometimes only a pretext. In other groups, different issues could have served the same purpose; for example, the workers appearing to members as uncaring. In both situations the dilemma may well be the same. The unspoken dilemma revolves around members' underlying wish to wrest power from the workers, on the one hand, and their need to ensure that the workers continue to care for them, on the other (Levine 1979, p.122).

In this example, the members accuse Clive of talking to them as if they were children, and of showing them no respect. Very often there is a grain of truth in the accusations. Yet, the protest in this example is expressed so vehemently, persistently, and unfairly that the workers have good reasons to look for an undercurrent that may be troubling members beyond the specific complaint. It is such an undercurrent, often called 'hidden agenda', that complicates and intensifies the dynamics.

The experience of this stage is often puzzling because, for quite a while, members willingly accept the very same behaviour about which they later complain. Only later on do they appear to experience the established authority of the workers as restrictive. It is then that members begin to feel 'patronised', or 'uncared for', but not before. This delay in complaining is probably the key to the meaning of members' unrest.

Ironically, if after a number of sessions the members do not complain about being powerless, the workers may have reasons to worry that members' sense of competence has not grown sufficiently to seek power for themselves. Yet, when the members do complain about the workers' power, the chances are that they feel competent enough to handle power themselves. Put in this context, the members' complaint is, paradoxically, a sign that the group-workers have done well. In this sense, the workers' demise is their own success. The workers' achievement is in enhancing the members' sense of competence.

Why are members caught up in such a complicated set of exchanges? This is the crux of the Authority crisis. A paradox surfaces as the members try to break loose of the parallel relationships established during the engagement phase. Smith and Berg (1987, pp. 133–139) call it 'the paradox of authority', and explain that:

> Taking the power that is available and using it often creates a vacuum, because it is experienced as depriving others of a scarce commodity … Individuals often refuse to accept or exercise the power that is available to them in a group simply to avoid the accusation of having stolen it from someone else (Smith and Berg 1987, p.134).

So, instead of risking competition with their peers, members often try to exercise power over their workers first. Of course, members still fear retaliation by the workers. This is why members tend to polarise their reactions: some members actually protect the workers, while others attack them ferociously. When the workers do not retaliate, members usually despair of these simple polarities and begin to search for new solutions.

The crisis can be judged as being resolved if it leads to specific alternatives being suggested – not by the workers, but by group members themselves (entries 56–59). Indeed, the constructive resolution of this crisis is the empowerment of the members. Inevitably, members' empowerment leads to revising the initial expectations about the use of power in the group: a normative shift takes place. The new norms create opportunities for more varied forms of influencing the group so that more members are able to exercise some degree of power.

Understanding the paradox of authority may help workers weather this storm constructively. Smith and Berg (1987, p.134) note that: 'One develops power as one empowers others.' The workers have to understand that their power depends on allowing members to take power from them.

Individual members themselves may benefit from this often painful experience too. In relation to Yalom's (1995, pp.69–105) curative factors, the experience of criticising the worker may be an important opportunity for catharsis, as in 'Expressing negative feelings towards the group leader' and 'Being able to say what was bothering me instead of holding it in.' Such direct expression may be related also to some aspects of interpersonal learning as input; for example, 'Learning that I sometimes confuse people by not saying what I really think.'

The workers' responses in this excerpt may not necessarily suit your own situation. Other ways exist which equally address this stormy dynamic. So, understanding the full dynamic may be the priority now.

Choosing the appropriate level
Abandoning the social level by re-defining the interpersonal one
Up to this session the members have resorted to parallel relationships; each member directly relating to the workers in parallel to the others. Inevitably, the workers have been charged with a great deal of authority. Questions have been directed to them, and answers have come from them. This excessively powerful position has been helpful at the beginning, but now it blocks the empowerment of the members.

To understand the need for change, it may be helpful to note that the workers' position of power has been sustained by the members deferring to the workers' judgement; that is, by relating to Jane and Clive mainly as 'the workers', which in turn has meant that the members have seen themselves mainly as just 'members'. These clearly defined positions have been grounded in the social roles established at the beginning. Although interspersed with interpersonal exchanges, the social level has been sustained up until now, and has perpetuated the centrality of the workers. Yet, now this level of social control seems to impede group members' expressions, and so a search for a different level begins.

You can see that the members' actual search begins at the already established social level – by talking about an anonymous reporter (entries 1–12). Members are still trying to uphold the well established social norms in spite of these norms leading them into an impasse. The workers could have gone along with that choice; for example, by again expanding on the role of the media in damaging members' self-esteem. Yet, now the workers do not settle for this social level, probably because they hear a certain ambivalence in the non-verbal cues that members convey.

These cues to ambivalence are not captured by a written transcript very easily. Yet, the unusually long silence with which the session starts, is one cue. Another is the members' apparent reluctance to express themselves directly about an anonymous reporter who is not even present in the room (entries 1–5). So, when David Thomas (entry 6) conveys despair about the reporter's style, Clive opts for a personal rather than a social response. Clive simply reflects back the 'painful' aspect (entry 7). The same choice is taken by Clive a few minutes later, when Moira Morris (entry 12) protests that: 'People talk, but when it comes to the walk...'. Even at this point, Clive or Jane could have tilted the conversation towards the social level by musing on the importance of doing what we say and saying what we do. Had the workers done so, no particular person would have been involved – the conversation would have remained at the social level.

Yet, Clive does not try to remain at the social level. Instead, Clive does try to enable more specific references to particular people, by simply asking (entry 13): 'Who else?' Gradually it turns out who else is involved: members' resentment is also directed towards Clive himself and later towards Jane.

Sensing a different level, Clive makes another choice when he responds to John Cook's protest about the fact that Clive has never had a child (entry 27). Clive could have ignored this question, but instead he briefly states (entry 28): 'I've never had a child of my own.' Such form of self-disclosure is not the only alternative open to Clive at this point. Clive could have also turned the focus to be on John himself, by inviting John to explore what John feels about having children. If Clive responded in this way, he would have deepened the experience and made it fully personal. Then, John's particular experiences of being a father would have been made the centre of attention. Yet, Clive does not choose to enter the personal level to such extent at this stage. Instead, Clive refers to a limited personal detail about himself; acknowledging the fact mentioned by John as correct (entry 28). Why this choice?

Faced with the Authority crisis, many workers know that unless it is resolved very little peer reliance and mutual aid will develop later. If Clive plunged so early into the personal level with John, the members would have learned that each of them in turn would be handled similarly by the workers. Therefore, the members might have not invested their energies in learning to work with one another. This is why both Clive and Jane avoid the totally personal level while also encouraging the group to move beyond the purely social one. The workers do so by expressing their personal feelings as these relate to the here-and-now of the group. You can see these comments in entries 23, and particularly 34: 'Yes, this is quite painful,' and also in entry 47. In this way, the workers model self-disclosure for the members. By infusing their social roles with personal comments the workers fully enter the interpersonal level. The workers' intention here is to signal to members that they may do the same; that is, members may also explore their own interpersonal positions. Indeed, the members seem to follow this lead, as suggested by their interpersonal involvement in entries 57 to 59.

> *During the Authority crisis the group is at a turning point: finally abandoning the purely Social level, and re-defining the boundaries to embrace Interpersonal experiences more fully.*

Processes

As mentioned in Chapter 2, the dynamics of crises are rather different from those of phases, and this is the first example of the transformational change involved in a crisis.

Amplifying

This episode actually begins with the stony silence that greets the workers as they begin the session. This frozen silence is a sign of the impasse. Indeed, the first three entries: 'Yes, well …'; 'Well what?'; 'Nothing really. Joyce is just…', are pretty empty utterances. These are further expressions of the members' sense of being stuck in an impasse. The members then begin to talk about what they saw on television the previous evening.

Clearly, a television programme is not the expected subject in a group that has agreed to examine how its members relate to their children. In systems terms, the topic is a deviation. Yet, the workers do not say that the topic is irrelevant.

Probably influenced by the unusual silence that greets them, the workers respond in ways that lead members to deviate from the agreed topic even more. You can see successive responses from the workers that aim to amplify the disturbing experience that members chose to express. Facilitating honest expression, Clive (entry 7) first communicates empathy with the feelings conveyed by David Thomas about the reporter. Jane (entry 10) follows Clive by reflecting back the bitterness implied in Joyce Cook's protest that the reporter has gone 'over the top' (entry 9).

As the intensity of members' feelings increases, Clive (entry 13) invites them to express themselves more specifically; to identify far more directly who the people are with whom they are so angry.

By acknowledging that: 'Something wasn't right last week', and by confirming that: 'We can talk about it too' (entry 20 and similarly in entry 23), Clive virtually invites members to criticise him and Jane. You can see that the members hesitate, and that Jane (entry 26) urges them to when she agrees: 'We'd better talk about it.'

These successively amplifying responses by the workers do lead to an outburst, expressed by John Cook: 'Well, to be honest, it was a bit much (to male worker). It's OK for you to talk, but let's face it, you've never had a child!' (entry 27) With this direct message, group members burst through the impasse and reveal their deeper concerns. Once the group bursts through the impasse, underlying issues can be clarified more easily.

Clarifying

When the criticism reaches its peak (entry 27: 'Let's face it, you've never had a child!'), the workers begin to help members make sense of it. In systems terms, they effect the feedback called here clarifying.

Clive bridges the difference between himself, as a worker, and the members by first confirming the fact of not having a child of his own (entry 28). Jane validates members' angry feelings by enquiring whether the central issue is members' feelings of being hurt by Clive (entry 31). As this proves to be the point, Clive then (entry 34) very fully bridges the difference between his powers as a worker and the validity of members' experiences of that power – acknowledging his own pain, reiterating the workers' duty to monitor risk to any child involved, and separating these issues from the members' criticism of the workers: 'Criticising us has nothing to do with your children being at risk. So, it has nothing to do with being on the Register either' (entry 34).

It seems that after that difference is bridged, members can express their deeper hurt, as Gerald Robinson says (entry 36): 'There's no need to rub it in', and Jean Robinson follows with: 'I'm no kid by any stretch of the imagination'. These quite personal references lead Clive to work further at bridging the difference between him and the members, when he says (entry 38): 'I don't see any of you as children, yet I seem to have hurt you'. With Jane's help (entries 40 and 43) Clive reaches the apparent core of the distress by communicating empathy with the members' experience of the workers 'coming across as patronising' (entry 45).

With the core concern out in the open, more practical ways of bridging the difference between workers and members are attempted. The workers acknowledge they cannot teach members how to raise their children (entry 47), and explain that they only do so when members either ask for direct advice or keep silent (entry 50). In this way, the workers re-define the problem as a group issue (entry 52). Such re-definition seems to help members search for their own ways of exercising power from now on.

Amplifying and Clarifying preoccupy the workers most of the time. Yet, some degree of Stabilising is needed too.

Stabilising

Only when some degree of clarity surfaces does the group attempt to re-structure its relationships (entries 53 to 59). Steering the group towards a new and desirable structural arrangement is a form of stabilising. In the example, the opening for re-structuring the use of power is signalled by Moira Morris (entry 53) who says: 'It'll have to change'. Clive sees this as a message that members are ready to work towards a different structure. So, Clive encourages re-contracting (entry 54). He is helped by Jane (entry 56) who reinforces Betty Carr's suggestion that each member will talk only when the member wants to. This new rule will be used to direct the range of members' contributions from this point onwards, and will be used to stabilise future exchanges among members.

Then members themselves suggest more changes and support these without the workers' involvement. This is the essence of the resolution of the Authority crisis: new solutions have to come from the members rather than the workers, so that members themselves effect the stabilising required.

Overall, this example begins with a focus on Amplifying disturbing experiences. Intensifying disturbing experiences is followed by making sense of the upheaval through Clarifying. Only when new meaning evolves is the group ready to resort to

Stabilising by re-structuring its relationships to enable wider distribution of power among the members.

Further implications for practice

Turning points

Choices open to the workers with regard to the level of group members' involvement have been already pointed out. Such choices also involve the process. The first choice occurs quite early: when David Thomas (entry 6) conveys his dismay at the way the reporter expressed himself. At that point, the workers could have seen David's message as a deviation from the agreed range of topics for this group: which is talking about raising children. So, the workers could have stabilised that digression; for example, by saying: 'that reporter does not appear to understand us. Perhaps we are better off talking among ourselves about handling our kids'. Such a response would have directed members back to the already established range of concerns. In systems terms such a response would have been a form of stabilising.

Yet, Clive's empathic response (entry 7) is aimed at amplifying David Thomas' underlying concern. A similar choice arises when Betty Carr (entry 19) says flatly: 'Better or worse, I don't mind. It wasn't right'. Clive could have chosen to help make it right for the group straight away; for example by saying: 'I can see it now, we'll have to accept it. What will make it right this week?' Such a direct attempt to put matters right again would have been a form of stabilising, as Clive would have retrieved the range of exchanges lost the previous week. You can see that Clive does not offer to stabilise members' expressions. Instead, Clive (entry 20) encourages the members to talk about the difficulty even more.

Throughout the example, the workers respond to successive potential turning points by amplifying the disturbing experiences conveyed by the members. Such choices are in the hands of each worker, and understanding the consequences of each may help each worker judge which one to follow.

Successive amplification is part of enabling transformational change, and this form of feedback is chosen by the workers in this example. When the workers consider step-by-step incremental changes to be more helpful, they can choose to respond with various forms of stabilising feedback.

Sustaining polarities

Bearing in mind the underlying ties between the polarities of amplifying and stabilising, as well as between the interpersonal and the personal levels, may help practice too. Let us take the first polarity; between *amplifying* and *stabilising*. Appreciating the tie between the two may lead practitioners to resort to both. Workers can do this by following the amplification of disturbing experiences with responses that stabilise incremental changes. Such changes usually enable the group to consolidate new solutions. Accordingly, the workers' responses during that last sequence (entries 54 and 56) are forms of stabilising; reinforcing the members' step-by-step problem-solving endeavours. Indeed, the resulting incremental changes can be seen in the example from entries 54 onwards. During these moments the group searches for changes that will be implemented in view of the previous explorations.

The second polarity is between the *interpersonal* and the *personal* levels. This tie may remind practitioners that the group may need some help in establishing the interpersonal level. Abandoning the social level may be threatening for members as at this level they feel most contained. Jumping into the deep end of the personal level may be equally daunting for members as they may fear that everything in their private worlds may begin to mix and mingle with everything else at this level. Dreading both changes, members often need to begin change by separating issues from one another at the interpersonal level. One way of helping the group with this is to fluctuate freely between the other two levels for a while. It is possible to make references to social concerns; for example, to the workers' roles as workers, and so – assure members that the social system, although not central anymore, is nevertheless still in place. Clive indicates this in entry 34 by saying: 'We do have to think about the register'. On the same occasion Clive also acknowledges the other side when he says: 'Yes, this is quite painful': expressing his own personal feelings quite directly. Such shuttling between the two levels makes sense if the aim is to shift the group's involvement towards blending the social and the personal into the interpersonal level.

Relevance of the Authority crisis

The same crisis may appear in some groups and not in others. Elsewhere (Manor 1997) I have already commented that the Authority crisis does not always surface even with groups that are very similar in their purpose and structure. The exact conditions which lead to this crisis are not fully known yet. As already mentioned, my own impression is that such a crisis tends to erupt when members become intensely involved in *highly ambivalent feelings*. Members' ambivalence is often about exposing what they perceive as internal divisions among themselves; for example, the division between competent and incompetent parents. Members often fear that when these divisions surface they will find themselves attacking and hurting one another. The consequences of these anticipated fights worry many group members, and members often hope that the worker will protect the group from these fights. Yet, while they seek such protection, members are also concerned about being too controlled. Many fear that they themselves may then appear as incapable of initiating anything significant.

The point is that internal divisions are sought as well as rejected, and the power of the worker to protect members is experienced as reassuring as well as demeaning. Ambivalence seems to rattle the group in regard to both issues.

The Authority crisis may be very relevant to groups that aim to explore the sharing of power; such as learning together how to assume responsibility for a child. In such situations, when the Authority crisis is seen to linger for too long, it may be possible to use the knowledge suggested here to help the group resolve this crisis safely.

Indeed, if you turn to the work of Benson (1987) again, you will see how the personal growth model does include an Authority crisis. Benson does not differentiate the conflict between group members and their worker from the conflicts among group members themselves. However, the beginning of Benson's 'control stage' is clearly concerned with members' relationships with the worker (Benson 1987, pp.103–106). In this, the initial period of Benson's control stage resembles the Authority crisis.

Some personal growth groups probably need the experience of the Authority crisis; possibly because of members' ambivalence about taking power for themselves and, at the same time, protecting themselves from competition with their peers. Such ambivalence does tend to arise among people who seek to find their own ways of sharing power with their peers. Demanding of the facilitator as this crisis may be, its contribution towards peer empowerment is then of paramount importance.

Yet, the Authority crisis cannot and should not be expected in each and every group. As you can see in O'Hara's (1988) educational model, no Authority crisis is expected in such groups. Indeed, it is not entirely clear that this crisis is particularly relevant to a group-oriented educational programme for prospective foster parents.

In between is the approach taken by Rose and Edleson (1987) for working with adolescents through their problem-solving model. These authors describe the stage of 'intervention' as led by the workers, and so seem to refer to this beginning in terms that resemble the present Engagement phase. When members show signs of dissatisfaction the workers gather the members around and ask them what can be improved (Rose and Edleson 1987, pp.285–296). By doing so the workers bypass the full eruption of the Authority crisis. Rather than handling the full blast of this crisis, Rose and

Edleson (1987, p.301) 'gradually eliminate the centralised leadership role' of the workers and encourage the youngsters to choose the topics themselves.

This gradual change prevents the eruption of the Authority crisis. Perhaps the authors assume that the needs of these youngsters are served best by gradually directing them towards a desirable range of peer relationships rather than leaving these adolescents to find their own ways of sharing power with their peers. The authors do not comment on this question.

Experiencing the Authority crisis may well be valuable for group members, but only when it is part of the purpose of their group. In these groups the Authority crisis is a prelude to entering the Empowerment phase.

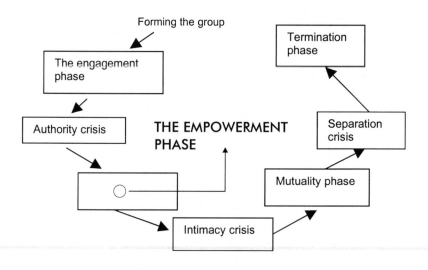

Figure 4.2 The Empowerment phase

Main features of this stage

The Empowerment phase gives rise to the paradox of identity: for each member to sustain her or his norms, each must defer to the group's norms. The Empowerment phase takes place mainly at the interpersonal level. During this phase clarifying is paramount, stabilising is actively pursued, and amplifying is relatively weak.

The example

1. Betty Carr: Well, we said we'd begin differently. So, how's everybody doing?

2. John Cook: Well yes, we did agree. We've had quite a good week, didn't we, Joyce?

3. David Thomas: (in a flat voice) Good for some.

4. Jean Robinson: No good for you, David?

5. Betty Carr: Let's just go round first, shall we?

6. Moira Morris: (irritated) At least there is some order HERE.

7. Jane: Sounds like there isn't much order THERE.

8. Assiff Khan: It's not easy to know …

9. Gerald Robinson: I don't know exactly how it's going.

(initial comments continue for a while)

10. David Thomas: (to Jane) Well, all these theories, they all mean you become a computer, everything planned. You really believe it can work?

11. Jane: It's a good question, David. You seem to ask me only as if I'm the only one who knows.

12. David Thomas: You are educated.

13. Jane: And other people here are educated too, in the university of life.

14. Clive: I wonder. How do other people go about planning what to do with the kids?

15. Moira Morris: They must know where they are. They can't grow up to expect everybody to run around them all the time.

16. Gerald Robinson: Not running around, but surely they're still kids…

17. David Thomas: They won't be kids for ever. Can't we let them enjoy it while it lasts?

18. Betty Carr: Sometimes I do let her run wild, but then there are certain things she just must do …

19. Moira Morris: I can't stand all this messing around. I don't remember us doing this when we were kids. We were raised properly: learning to stick to plans does you no harm later.

20. David Thomas: I don't know. I LIKE my kid being a kid, he's such fun, but last Sunday he really was out of order.

21. Moira Morris: I hope you don't mind me saying so, David, but perhaps that's because he never knows what order is in the first place.

22. David Thomas: Order, order – I get so much of it at work. Home is not work, and my boy isn't a worker yet, thank God. Home is not work, home is to feel relaxed. I don't want to come home and continue to feel like I'm at work.

23. Moira Morris: Of course not. At home we care for each other. So, we plan everything in advance. This way everybody is content, not like work.

24. David Thomas: Planning every detail is terrible. What sort of caring is this? Never do what you feel now, not three days ago? How can you really care?

25. Clive: It seems to me that Moira does, and you do too.

26. Joyce Cook: We all care for our kids. I'm sure …

27. Jean Robinson: Exactly what do we mean by 'caring'?

28. Jane: It seems the details are different for different parents.

29. Assiff Khan: But surely there is a difference. Some believe in respect and good behaviour. Others want to have fun with their kids and do their own thing too.

30. Jane: And the funny side is that, as far as we know, there's no evidence that one way is better than the other.

31. Moira Morris: Apart from so many youngsters misbehaving!

32. David Thomas: They misbehave not because of having had some fun, but because their parents don't get involved enough.

33. Jane: Yet parents who go for planning and discipline are very involved.

34. David Thomas: Are you saying that I'm not involved?

35. Clive: Difficult, this one. Perhaps others can help too.

36. Betty Carr: As I see it, you are both involved, but ... well ... perhaps in two different ways.

37. Gerald Robinson: One is like being a mate, and the other like being a teacher.

38. David Thomas: Maybe I'm the matey one, but I can tell you: there's a lot of teaching which I do there. He learns what playing fair is ...

39. Jane: So, perhaps it's not either or, perhaps ...

40. Moira Morris: A child must learn to follow rules. Later on she'll find that not all the rules are fair, by golly, I can teach her something about that, but she has to play by the rules!

41. Clive: It seems there are many different ways of making sure a child is prepared for life. Can we, in this group, live with this? Come to think about it, we too are different from one another: some are black, some are white, some men, some women. On some points each has a different outlook.

42. Joyce Cook: But we seem to argue a lot today.

43. Jane: You sound worried about this, Joyce.

44. Joyce Cook: Well, it used to be more cosy here.

45. Jane: Cosy, but perhaps less involved? I felt that today we argued more and yet we also got more involved with one another, particularly Moira and David. There's another thing. You see, some parents run into difficulties with their kids exactly because they are convinced that there is one and only one way of being a good parent. This particular way does not really suit them, but they are hooked on it. So, they always feel they aren't good enough parents. Then they get edgy, frustrated, and even angry. Then they, well, sometimes, hit the kid.

46. Jean Robinson: Like the white way is the right way.

47. Jane: Possibly. For me the most important thing in this group is not really teaching you THE WAY of being a good parent, but much more finding how different parents can be good parents and which approach would be best for each of you.

48. Clive: It's the talking about it together, and the listening, isn't it?

49. Betty Carr: Well, I suppose – like swapping notes ...

50. David Thomas: (smiling) Well, Moira and I certainly swapped some notes today.

51. Moira Morris: (calmly) It was good to speak my mind for a change.

This then, is the story so far. Let us see the themes contained in the contents.

Contents: Group themes and dilemmas

As explained in Chapter 2, during the Empowerment phase members work to separate themselves from one another so they can remain connected.

The underlying theme of this episode emerges towards entries 20 and 21: what is caring for children? What sort of order children need? What it means to be involved with them? What is the parent's responsibility? All these questions relate to norms about raising children, and the moral principles behind these norms.

David Thomas speaks for one set of norms: 'I don't want to come home and continue to feel like I'm at work' (entry 22), 'Planning every detail is terrible' (entry 24), (children) 'misbehave … because their parents don't get involved enough' (entry 32). David's view is that preparing a child for life is best done by involving the child in fun and practical issues. Gerald Robinson labels this 'being a mate' (entry 37).

Moira Morris speaks for a different view: for her, caring is when we 'plan everything in advance. This way everybody is content' (entry 23). 'Learning to stick to plans does you no harm' (entry 19), since 'a child must learn to follow rules' (entry 40). Her approach is of the parent as 'a teacher' (entry 37).

Such divisions are quite common after the Authority crisis. Though members begin to feel equal to one another, they also realise that they are certainly not identical. Now members realise that they are facing a new challenge: how to handle these differences.

As explained in Chapter 2; through power relations, various experiences can be readily separated from one another. This separation is handled by formulating principles that often appear incompatible, as are the principles of being 'mates' versus being 'teachers'. Then a struggle often ensues between the proponents of each principle. A period of wheeling and dealing follows: who will speak for how long? Whose opinions will prevail? Whose suggestions will be merely acknowledged? Which subjects and experiences will be considered relevant in this group? Who will be 'in' and who will feel 'out'? This period is similar to Tuckman and Jensen's (1977) stage of 'norming'.

Such a struggle can be seen in the present example too. On the face of it, the group is debating different and separate models of being parents: 'mates' or 'teachers'. By implication, if one model is right, the other must be wrong. When such an argument becomes a win–lose exchange, the contest between 'mates' and 'teachers' is often associated with an underlying struggle for power which may pre-occupy the group for quite a while. To help the group with this struggle the workers suggest a wider angle. The workers raise the question whether there is one and only one model of child rearing at all.

Jane, the worker, raises the possibility that there is no single model (entry 45), and that each parent must find his or her own way (entry 47). This new view has a crucial effect on the group's dynamics. If, within certain limits of safety and dignity, there is no one way that is always superior to the others, no member can claim to be a superior parent. If no member can be superior, there is not much point in competing over being the best parent. Therefore, there is less room for a pecking order among the members. As Clive, the worker, suggests, all that remains is 'the talking about it together, and the listening' (entry 48). Betty Carr signals that this new level may be accepted when she talks about 'swapping notes' (entry 49). Consequently, while neither David nor Moira are pressed to change their views, a third over-riding norm emerges, which also connects members: swapping notes by talking together and listening. The members seem to realise the paradox of identity (Smith and Berg 1987, pp.90–95): for each member to sustain her or his norms; in our case, those of a 'teacher' or a 'mate', each must also defer to the group's norms; in our case, swapping notes by talking together and listening.

The importance of empowering group members can be explained by referring to Yalom's (1995, pp.69–195) curative factors. If the paradox of identity is central then a number of curative factors seem relevant. Among them will be: insight – particularly 'Learning that I react to some people or situations unrealistically (with feelings that somehow belong to earlier periods in my life)'; group cohesiveness as in 'Belonging to and being accepted by a group'; universality as in 'Seeing that I was just as well off as others'; interpersonal learning as 'input' expressed in the phrase 'Other members honestly telling me what they think of me'; and interpersonal learning as 'output', conveyed in 'improving my skills in getting along with people'.

How can the workers contribute to developing such an enabling culture? Of course there are quite a number of ways. Still further aspects of the dynamics may be a good guide.

Choosing the appropriate level: The interpersonal level expanded

You may have realised that the workers are faced with certain choices in this example. After David Thomas asks Jane if she believes theories can really work (entry 10), the workers can choose to respond at the social level. They can develop a conversation about theories of parenthood and their application to daily life. This could have been appropriate at the very beginning – during the Engagement phase. At that early stage members might have benefited from an overview; a purely social perspective, of parenthood. The workers' judgement in this example is that the members have moved on by now, and that the discussion can be more personal.

On the other hand, the workers can also choose to deepen the experiences and make them purely personal. For example, when David Thomas (entry 24) talks with such passion about 'caring', the workers can communicate empathy and suggest connections to David's own earlier experiences of being cared for. Yet, the workers do neither.

Instead, Jane comments on these personal experiences in the context of being in the social role of a parent. She says: 'It seems the details are different for different *parents*' (entry 28). Again, in entry 40, Moira Morris expresses very strong feelings about conforming to unfair rules. The workers can deepen this by asking her about any unfairness in her own life. Yet, the workers do not choose to do this. Clive (entry 41) still responds to living with differences. In the second part of Chapter 5, you will see that the workers do take up the deeper personal issues indicated by both David and Moira, but for now they wait.

Why this delay? The reason is quite simple. If the workers really believe that the members must learn to help one another, they must first offer them opportunities to practise this form of mutual aid. Deepening experiences to the very personal level so early may leave most of the facilitative work in the hands of the workers, as members may soon settle for this pattern. Then, during each session one or two of them will open up relatively deep personal issues, and expect to be helped only by the workers. As a result, mutual help among the members may not develop. This is why, at this stage, the workers opt for the middle ground. The middle ground is neither purely social nor deeply personal. This ground involves individual differences such as those between David Thomas and Moira Morris. Yet, these differences relate to the ways these members handle certain social roles; those of parents. The ways individual differences influence people in their social roles are structured at the interpersonal level.

This structure often seems to serve an undeclared function. As long as the interpersonal pattern is maintained, experiences associated with each principle can be kept separate from one another, and so – the distance between members who believe in each can be readily regulated. At the same time, confirming that no single principle is superior ensures some connection among the members.

As mentioned in Chapter 1, often the interpersonal level can be sustained by resorting to the pattern of a network; where each member is sufficiently separated from the others while the workers encourage connections as they are free to be closer to some and more distant from others at different points in time.

Overall, the Empowerment phase takes place mainly at the Interpersonal level.

Processes

Clarifying

Many of the workers' responses are forms of clarifying during this stage. Increasingly, the members themselves raise the contents that are relevant to them, and so the workers can focus on clarifying the communication about these contents. You can see how the members themselves start the session now, and how the workers wait for quite a while until they feel their response is needed. When the workers do speak, it is first to communicate empathy with Moira Morris (entry 7). Apart from a brief yet important intervention between entries 11 and 14, the workers then wait for even longer. Only when members begin to split their perceptions too rigidly do the workers judge that they are needed again. This point is reached when David Thomas uses very extreme terms such as '...terrible. What sort of caring is this?' (entry 24) to refer to the 'teaching approach' advocated by Moira Morris. Clive responds by reaching for 'caring' as a feeling link between the two, when he says (entry 25): 'It seems to me that Moira does (care), and you do too'. Jane follows this soon by reaching for a difference when she says (entry 28): 'It seems the details are different for different parents'. Jane then reaches for a link again, in entry 30: 'And the funny side is that, as far as we know, there's no evidence that one way is better than the other'. Such shuttling between the common ground and the differences among members has to continue for a while because members are still trying to split up perceptions too rigidly. So, in entry 33, Jane reaches for 'involvement' as a feeling link again, by saying: 'Yet parents who go for planning and discipline are very involved.' You can see that Jane becomes quite explicit about the need to connect polarities when she very openly reaches for a link in entry 39, saying: 'So, perhaps it's not either or, perhaps …'. This type of clarifying is very typical of workers' involvement during the Empowerment phase.

Stabilising

As is the case with clarifying, the workers wait during this stage too until they are really needed. During the Empowerment phase it is often helpful to steer group members towards relating to one another more than to the workers. You can see the first stabilising response in entry 11. When David Thomas (entry 10) tries to involve Jane in discussing the relevance of theories, Jane re-directs the message to the rest of the group, by saying (entry 11): 'You seem to ask me only as if I'm the only one who knows'. Jane reinforces the re-direction in entry 13, and Clive makes it explicit in entry 14: 'How do other people go about planning what to do with the kids?' Yet, the workers' response is minimal. A period of somewhat heated exchanges among the members follows and the workers do not interfere (entries 15 to 24).

The need to stabilise again arises later – when the workers judge that it is better for more members to be involved. In entry 35, Clive yet again re-directs the message to more of the members by saying: 'Difficult this one. Perhaps others can help too'. Then the workers very explicitly resort to stabilising when they verbalise group norms. Verbalising norms can be seen in entry 41, when Clive says: 'It seems there are many ways of making sure a child is prepared for life. Can we, in this group, live with this?' Jane grasps this mantle even more firmly when she voices group achievements in entry 45, saying: 'I felt that today we argued more and yet also got more involved with one another.'

Then, Jane straightaway continues to verbalise group norms by talking about the self-defeating nature of believing that there is only one model for raising children. Jane continues to verbalise these norms in entry 47; talking about the advantages of exploring many models of child rearing. Clive summarises this in entry 48, by saying: 'It's the talking about it together, and the listening, isn't it?' Verbalising these pluralistic norms is a way of steering group members towards a pluralistic peer culture, and in this sense is a form of stabilising too.

Amplifying

You will have probably noticed that no attempt is made by the workers to intensify any deviation now. On the contrary, David Thomas' deviation from the norm of peer involvement (entry 10) is re-directed by Jane back to the members. Some of the workers' empathic responses could have amplified members' concerns, but these are not followed up in close succession. So, the effect of empathy remains that of clarifying. Overall, during the Empowerment phase amplifying disturbing experiences is very weak.

Altogether, during the Empowerment phase Clarifying is paramount, Stabilising is actively pursued, and Amplifying is very weak.

Further implications for practice

Turning points

Potential turning points among levels have been discussed already when choosing the appropriate level has been explored. These points more or less correspond to choices made with regard to the process too. As far as processes are concerned, a potential turning point arises in entry 6; when Moira Morris appears so tense about maintaining order. Jane (entry 7) does respond empathically, but does not persevere. Jane could have returned to Moira's expression; successively communicating empathy to amplify it, but instead Jane restricts her response to a form of clarifying, and lets the group take the exchanges elsewhere.

The choice to let go of Moira's tense expression is influenced by the main aim of the Empowerment phase. Had Jane amplified Moira's concern, the exploration might have extended to the personal level. Yet, as noted before, at this stage the aim is to enhance member-to-member exchanges at the interpersonal level, more than deepening the exploration by one member alone.

A similar choice occurs in entry 24, when David Thomas protests so very intensely that: 'Never do what you feel now' cannot be caring. Of course the workers could have amplified this highly charged message and could have facilitated exploration at the personal level; for example, of David's past memories of being cared for. Indeed, when the Mutuality phase is discussed later, you will see how the workers do just that. But, here we are still in the Empowerment phase, and the workers feel that David's involvement is best enhanced at the interpersonal level. The workers make this choice because they hold the view that at this level David may develop his relationships with other group members more fully. This is why Clive responds by reaching for a feeling link between David Thomas and Moira Morris (entry 25); that is, Clive resorts to stabilising.

Sustaining polarities

Focusing on the interpersonal level during the empowerment phase means that exchanges may well touch upon its components: the social and the personal levels. Yet, when the interpersonal level is the priority the workers respond so that each of the other two levels can serve as points of reference rather than major concerns. In the example, members refer to social principles of child rearing (see entries 15, 16, 22, 37,40), but soon explore these from their own personal experiences. In the same vein, members do refer to personal experiences (see entry 19), but draw on these to explore their own roles of being parents (entries 18, 20, 21, 36, 38). In both instances, the members refer to the social as well as the personal level to inform their involvement at the interpersonal level.

As far as the polarities of process are concerned, it may be helpful to remember that *the Empowerment phase tends to neglect amplifying disturbing experiences, while stabilising is often emphasised.*

This polarity between stabilising and amplifying often underpins the debate between directive and facilitative practitioners. In the present example, you can see that from entry 41 onwards, the workers themselves verbalise the group norms they consider helpful; and so, are rather directive. While doing so, the workers are emphasising stabilising quite openly. Yet, in other groups it may be very important that group members work through such norms without so much guidance from the workers.

It seems that the difference is only a matter of degree. In the present example, a risk may be involved in allowing a great deal of time until members reach a pluralistic acceptance of the differences among themselves. Meanwhile, some members may feel forced to conform to norms that do not suit their circumstances. When such parents conform to unsuitable norms they may mishandle situations and harm their children.

If there is a risk that polarised norms may lead to some harm; as may be the case with parents who are too quick to respond to their children's behaviour, the workers may follow one of the approaches. It may then stand to reason to suggest the enabling new norms quite explicitly, and thereby adopt a more directive style. Yet, if no harm can come from waiting until members work out their own pluralistic culture, a different stance may be taken by the workers. In such situations the workers may opt for a more facilitative style, and so they may communicate empathy with members' tentative, exploratory, and even contradictory ideas for quite a while. In so doing, workers may intensify members' doubts and even confusion – experiences that can be quite disturbing to members. In other words, the workers may effect some degree of amplifying in such safe situations.

It is hoped that the present evolving framework will encourage such judicial applications.

Relevance of the Empowerment phase

The emphasis on increasing members' competence in handling peer relationships may be very attractive to workers who consider empowerment the central issue in all relationships. Of course empowerment is understood in quite a number of ways. Enhancing members' problem-solving skills may not in itself give them powers to change all the conditions in their environment. Yet, problem-solving skills can empower youngsters to negotiate their needs with adults and with their peers more effectively.

This rationale seems to lie behind the approach taken by Rose and Edleson (1987) in their work with children and adolescents. Such an emphasis is apparent during the latter period of the stage these authors call 'intervention'. That period seems to be dedicated to encouraging the youngsters to raise individual problem situations and explore alternative solutions while increasingly taking a more active part in leading the group (Rose and Edleson 1987, pp.293–303). Indeed, it seems that this stage preoccupies such groups for most of their duration.

A similar range of experiences is described by Benson (1987) while working with adults in personal growth groups. The latter period of Benson's 'control stage' is dedicated to encouraging members to learn systematic problem-solving, creative decision-making, and team collaboration (Benson 1987, pp.115–122). Yet, these personal growth groups do not appear to spend all their time at this phase. Presumably, other matters are on members' minds, which propel them to move beyond power and leadership issues.

Vital as it is, even peer empowerment is not always an important goal. You can see this in the educational model discussed by O'Hara (1988) where all the sessions are led by the workers as they prepare adults for the tasks of fostering.

Within the present evolving framework, practitioners are invited to clarify the relevance of the Empowerment phase for each group afresh.

Whether or not the group engages in the phase of empowerment, in some groups more personal issues may then surface. Yet, under certain conditions groups have to go through the Intimacy crisis before members can safely explore these more intimately confusing concerns.

CHAPTER 5

Intimacy Crisis and the Mutuality Phase

Two stages will be demonstrated in this chapter: the Intimacy crisis and the Mutuality phase.

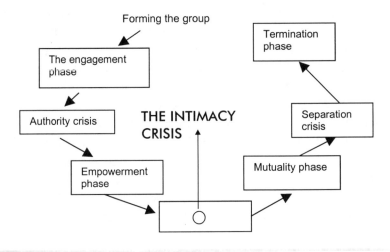

Figure 5.1 The Intimacy crisis

Main features of this stage

The Intimacy crisis gives rise to the paradox of boundaries: While boundaries enable us to act they also restrict our action. During this crisis the group discards the confines of the interpersonal level, and opens-up the personal level to allow a wider range of experiences in the group. The Intimacy crisis first involves a great deal of amplifying and actively engages the group in clarifying. Later, this crisis calls for emphasising stabilising.

The example

Because of the intimate nature of the experiences, this extract will be slightly longer than others.

After some weeks passed in the Empowerment phase, the following events erupted:

1. John Cook: Well, yes, last week we talked about that men–women thing.

2. Assiff Khan: I've been thinking about it. We don't really have to go on like our parents did, but...

3. Jane: But, when we try it differently...?

4. John Cook: (hesitant and tense) I did try! I thought I was meant to tell off the kid.

5. David Thomas: (teasingly) Wow John, you've become the baddy now.

6. John Cook: As I've said, it's not that which I mind...

7. Clive: Something seems not to have worked.

8. Joyce Cook: It was all right, really, he did try to pull his weight. He did tell her off.

(John Cook stares at the floor silently)

9. Betty Carr: Come on John, something did not work?

10. John Cook: I don't know anymore. I thought I did the right thing.

    (to Jane) Well, to tell you the truth; it's OK for you to say that men should take care of the kids more, but when they do, the reactions...

11. Jane: Yes, it's the reactions. Whose reactions, John?

12. Joyce Cook: John, is it me? I was chuffed by what you did.

13. John Cook: Were you? You certainly have strange ways of showing it.

14. Clive: Perhaps this is it? John, how did Joyce look to you?

15. John Cook: Well, you know, that look on her face, as if I'd done something... She said it was all right, but she looked worried, almost angry, I don't know...

16. Jane: Joyce, do you remember? Did you feel angry or worried at what John had done?

17. Joyce Cook: Me? Oh, no! I wasn't angry!

18. Jane: You were pleased at John pulling his weight.

19. Joyce Cook: Yes I was.

20. Jane: I wonder, sometimes we feel more than one thing at the same time, particularly when something new happens, like John disciplining Ruth. Maybe, I just wonder Joyce, did you have any other feelings suddenly coming up? Not that you expected them, but still – any other feelings?

(silence all round)

21. Joyce Cook: Well, yes it was a bit strange, I'd never seen John like that, I mean raising his voice... Suddenly I got quite worried.

22. Clive: While feeling good about the change John had made, you suddenly got also quite anxious.

23. Joyce Cook: Well, I suppose. If there is one thing about John it's his kindness, but seeing him like that... (her face frowns and her voice chokes)

24. Jane: So, you do want John to tell Ruth off and when he does, you worry. Doesn't make sense, does it? (pause, Joyce shakes her head, in the negative) Joyce, this may sound crazy to you, and I may be totally wrong, but do you remember? Was there anybody else in your *own* life, maybe years ago, who had frightened you with shouting?

25. John Cook: Joyce had not been married to anybody else before me ...

26. Jane: No, not a previous husband.

(long and tense silence. Joyce's gaze is fixed at the floor, other members are watching and listening intently)

27. Joyce Cook: (voice choked, close to tears) Well ... he was ... it was awful ...

28. Clive: He was awful ...

29. Betty Carr: Who was he, Joyce, please tell us.

30. Joyce Cook: I know he worked hard. I know he tried his best to provide.

31. Clive: That man who worked hard and was trying his best to provide for you was also awful to you. (Joyce Cook bursts into heavy crying) The same father was both, and it hurts very much even thinking about it.

32. Joyce Cook: It's ... the shouting ... the belting (cries shaking with fear) ... so terrifying ... every Thursday night ... after the pub ...

33. Jane: You feel frightened. That big man will come in again, yell all over the place, beat you up.

(Joyce sobs for quite a while. The rest of the members warmly lean forward towards her)

34. Betty Carr: I think ... (voice trembling) ... I think it is terrible. It is something ... I think ...

35. Clive: Betty, there's something here that you recognise?

36. David Thomas: (anxiously) Clive! Really!

37. Clive: Something you want to think about? Here?

38. David Thomas: Clive – really there's no need to ... (even more anxious) stop it ... you are just bringing everybody to tears.

39. Jane: Tears are very difficult for some of us.

40. David Thomas: Well, we can't all go weak. We have the kids to take care of.

41. Moira Morris: All this may go too far.

42. Clive: Is it also too far for Betty? Perhaps we should hear Betty too.

43. Betty Carr: Tears are the easy part.

44. Jane: Tears are not difficult for you, Betty, but ...

45. Betty Carr: Understanding is ... (sharply) never mind!

46. Jane: (warmly) I mind, Betty. What do you want to say? What about understanding?

47. Betty Carr: Look, it doesn't matter, it's too much.

48. John Cook: Too much for whom, Betty – you or us?

49. Betty Carr: Well, it's not new to me, but ... well, that's how it is.

50. Joyce Cook: Some things are difficult to explain to others.

51. Moira Morris: We shouldn't pressurise Betty.

52. Jane: Betty – do you feel under pressure?

53. Betty Carr: It's not pressure, it's more ...

54. John Cook: Confusion?

55. Betty Carr: Well, to be honest, by now I am not confused about it, but for you ...

56. Clive: We may get confused. Well, we may. What's so awful about us getting confused?

57. Betty Carr: You may get the ...

58. Jane: Wrong idea?

59. Betty Carr: Well, it was quite strange to me.

60. Jane: And very confusing, then?

61. Betty Carr: It WAS. VERY confusing.

62. Clive: Betty, do you think you can say just a bit about what it actually was?

63. Betty Carr: It was like Jekyll and Hyde: when he was in she was all sweet and smiling, but when he was out ... (hesitates)

64. Jane: She was your Mum?

65. Betty Carr: Well when Dad was out, she would go strange ... smoking a lot, getting at me for the smallest thing ... (trembling a little) Once she, well she hit me (looking at the floor as if guilty). I put on lipstick before going out. She went mad, swearing at me that I was a whore. I don't know what hurt more: the punch, or the words.

66. Jane: I can understand how painful it was for you.

67. Betty Carr: Yes, but that was only ... (curling in her chair)

68. Clive: There was more to it?

69. Betty Carr: It turned out there was ... (looking at the window) ... it took me years to work it out. Maybe it's not important anymore.

70. John Cook: And maybe it is. You seem to feel it.

71. Betty Carr: It's difficult to work out.

72. Moira Morris: Perhaps we can help.

73. Betty Carr: I don't know. (silent for a while) It turned out that he had told her ... before getting married, you see, he had told her that sometimes he went off with ... that ... OK: that he was gay.

(silence all round)

74. Clive: (reassuringly) He had told her he was gay. Yet, they got married.

75. Betty Carr: I know, it's weird.

76. David Thomas: Not so weird for me.

77. Betty Carr: Later on she said she had hoped to change him. She thought that if she tried harder ...

78. Jane: Tried harder to do what?

79. Betty Carr: I suppose she felt it was her failure. She felt a failure as a woman I suppose, but ...

80. Clive: But at the time you could not possibly know that, could you?

81. Betty Carr: (looking straight towards Clive) I did not know any of these things: men going off with other men. It's difficult to ...

82. Jane: It's difficult for you to understand this even now, Betty?

83. Betty Carr: It's ... I don't know ...

84. Clive: How about the rest of the group? How difficult is it for us?

85. Assiff Khan: It's not so difficult. This does happen.

86. Jean Robinson: We need to remember that at that time nobody would talk about such things.

(conversations continue with mixed reactions)

87. Clive: I am glad we, in this group, CAN talk about it all.

This example is, of course, still condensed and incomplete. In real life the Intimacy crisis lasts for a longer period, and has to include further aspects. Still, the essentials are there. Let us see the dilemmas contained therein.

Contents: Group themes and dilemmas

For the present purpose, only major themes can be identified. Ostensibly, the example begins with shifting parental responsibilities between a husband and a wife: John and Joyce Cook. Yet, Joyce Cook's reactions to her husband raising his voice puzzled him, and so the interpersonal change both husband and wife want cannot be achieved. When attention is paid to Joyce's reactions, her ambivalence surfaces. As Clive (entry 22) points out: 'While feeling good about the change John had made, you suddenly got also quite anxious'. The associated impasse is identified by Jane (entry 24): 'So, you do want John to tell Ruth off and when he does, you worry. Doesn't make sense, does it?' The couple reach an impasse.

To break through this impasse, it seems necessary to venture into more personal experiences. Indeed, personal experiences from Joyce's past surface very powerfully now: memories of her father's violent behaviour shake Joyce to the core.

These memories seem to reverberate through the group. Sometimes one member's experiences echo in another, but do not necessarily mirror them fully. In the example, Betty Carr identifies with Joyce Cook, but Betty has been harbouring frightening and confusing memories related not to her father's physical aggression, but to her mother's hostility towards her. Yet, a theme is shared between the two women.

The main point here is the dilemma involved in breaking through the interpersonal boundaries previously established by the group. The struggle begins when Joyce Cook insists on holding back her conflicting reactions to John disciplining Ruth. The difficulty Joyce experiences stems not only from remembering frightening experiences. Joyce is also thrown back by the realisation that these painful memories, at the personal level, are suddenly connected with their opposite – the pleasing changes made by John at the interpersonal one. You can see that sometimes Joyce Cook talks as a parent who is searching for a new way of handling her child, and at other times Joyce talks as an adult whose childhood memories have come back to haunt her.

Such struggles with conflicting themes may be inevitable; particularly when each theme is embedded at a different level. Smith and Berg (1987, pp.102–108) point out the paradox involved in crossing the boundaries between levels. Smith and Berg explain that: 'boundaries simultaneously make it possible for a group to take action and limit action by what the boundaries define' (Smith and Berg 1987, p.103). In our example, drawing the boundaries so that only interpersonal issues are explored has been helpful during the Empowerment phase. These boundaries have enabled members to explore their competences of acting in the roles of parents towards their children. Yet, the same boundaries have also limited the exploration, as the interpersonal boundaries excluded personal experiences that interfered with competent interpersonal functioning.

Now members begin to sense the emerging paradox. Members begin to realise that the constraints of the interpersonal level prevent them from achieving further goals – those influenced by the personal level.

By itself, opening up the personal level can be of value to members. If we relate these experiences to Yalom's (1995, pp.69–105) curative factors, we may consider group cohesiveness; as in 'Revealing embarrassing things about myself and still being accepted by the group' to be enhanced. Universality; as in 'Learning that others had parents and background as unhappy or mixed up as mine', may be promoted too, and opportunities for catharsis; for example when 'Getting things off my chest', may well become available. Identification among members may arise when 'Seeing that others could reveal embarrassing things and take other risks and benefit from it helped me do the same'.

Workers can help the group handle the dilemmas of boundaries by validating the confusion created when levels of involvement change.

Choosing the appropriate level: From the interpersonal to the personal

When the Intimacy crisis follows the Empowerment phase, it can be expected to begin at the interpersonal level. The interpersonal level can be seen in Assiff Khan's early comment (entry 2): 'We don't really have to go on like our parents did, but …'. Here you can see a member exploring his own way of negotiating gender roles; the 'men–women thing' mentioned just before. Indeed, the conversations remain at the interpersonal level until entry 20. Only then does Jane allude to a different level: 'Any other feelings suddenly coming up? Not that you expected them …'.

This reference, to an unexpected range of feelings, is an attempt to see whether members feel the need to open up the established boundaries now. Jane is gauging members' readiness to share feelings that up to now have been considered less relevant; that is, 'unexpected'. In systems terms, Jane's response is at the interface; the boundary point, between the interpersonal and the personal levels. Indeed, the following entries; 21 and 22; about the experience being 'a bit strange', take place at this area where the two levels combine to provoke considerable unease.

Due to the workers' responsiveness, the conversations do indeed enter the personal level soon after. This happens when Joyce Cook fully and painfully shares her memories of a violent father, during entries 25–33. These personal revelations reverberate in the group with such force that Betty Carr begins to remember her own personal past too. In entry 34, she begins to struggle with the disclosure of her own personal memories, and is encouraged to do so by Clive (entry 35). Yet, a barrier is put up by some members. David Thomas (entry 38) protests that Clive is 'just bringing everybody to tears', and Moira Morris (entry 41) supports David Thomas, who, in entry 40, explains that: 'We can't all go weak. We have the kids to take care of'.

My practice experience is that such blocking of the personal level is quite common. More often than not, this form of resistance reflects the members' ambivalence.

On the one hand members do want to allow a wider range of experiences and are ready to open up the group boundaries. This can be seen by their responsive attentiveness to Joyce Cook. On the other, the members also want to close down the group boundaries so that they feel safe enough. So, members resort to reasons, such as the need to be strong for the children's sake, which justify closing off the personal boundaries. In doing so, members return to the level experienced as the opposite; the interpersonal level. At this level members are separate individuals who are also the same – all are parents to children who must regard all of them as strong all the time.

Faced with such further blocking, the workers could have amplified Betty Carr's reluctance and the members' protection of her; for example, by pointing out that it may be too much to encourage every member to share feelings as deep as those disclosed by Joyce Cook. In the example, the workers probably estimate that by now, the resistance to further disclosure is not as intense as it has been before Joyce Cook broke through the impasse.

Now the workers take a more direct approach. Jane communicates empathy with Betty Carr's message that: 'Tears are the easy part' (entry 43), and then a number of exchanges follow. These exchanges meander between two levels: one level is of rather vague social generalisations; such as: 'What about understanding?', 'It's too much', and 'Well it's not new to me ... well, that's how it is'. The other level includes allusions to rather personal experiences, such as: 'Some things are difficult to explain to others' or 'By now I am not confused about it, but for you ...' (entries 45–55). Members often shuttle between levels several times when they explore the interface between them. Clive (entry 56) identifies the bewildering feeling involved in exploring the interface when he wonders: 'What's so awful about us getting confused?'

Permission to be confused is often necessary, and approving of confusion is one way of validating the experience of opening up boundaries. You can see that such reassurance is needed. Only after Betty Carr is assured by both workers that her confusion is a valid experience, can she fully share memories of a very confusing mother and an unusual marital arrangement between her parents. With these disclosures elaborated, Betty Carr fully enters the personal level. Yet, Betty still seems to need help.

The rest of the episode is taken up by the workers reassuring Betty Carr that she is understood by them as well as by the rest of the group. Shared understanding among group members is the most powerful form of supporting communication in areas of taboo. When such supportive culture is established, the personal level is made fully available to all members.

Altogether, during the Intimacy crisis the group loosens up its Interpersonal boundaries and establishes the Personal level as the major area for future explorations.

Processes

Amplifying

You may have noticed that when John Cook begins hesitantly: 'I did try! I thought I was meant to tell off the kid,' (entry 4), the workers are faced with a choice. They can pursue the behavioural goal: praising John for reprimanding his daughter rather than leaving it all to Joyce.

Yet, a simple behavioural response would not have fully addressed this situation. John's staring at the floor in response to Joyce's acknowledgement (entry 8) does not square up with his behavioural achievement; it stands out. In systems terms, John's bodily expression is a 'deviation' from the expected reactions of sitting upright and expressing satisfaction or even pride. This discrepancy leads the workers to amplify John's deviation. Clive first communicates empathy: 'Something seems not to have worked' (entry 7). The word 'something' refers to John's bodily expression: the disturbing message which deviates from the expected ones, and this is followed rapidly by group members in entry 9: 'Come on John, something did not work?' Jane (entry 11) then draws out the hidden message: The reactions. Whose reactions?

Now the workers sense that much more has to be brought to the surface. So, the workers focus on Joyce Cook's reactions; communicating empathy with Joyce in close succession during entries 26, 28, and 31, and particularly 33, as Joyce struggles to express her most distressing memories.

During the rest of this episode amplifying is offered far less actively. This is where the Intimacy crisis may differ from the Authority crisis. During the Authority crisis, all group members focus on one issue: the powers held by the workers. The Authority crisis erupts at a stroke as this crisis has one clear focus: the workers. The Authority crisis may be likened to a house of cards: you pull one card and the whole structure will collapse. The Intimacy crisis may be different as each member has his or her own routes to the personal level.

Various members may resonate with the one who discloses personal experiences first. In the example, Betty Carr seems to identify with Joyce Cook and follow her suit. Yet, each member is ambivalent about different contents. Betty Carr is ambivalent about her mother's violence, while Joyce Cook is ambivalent about being abused by her father. The shared ambivalence about past abuse is individualised according to its different sources. Thus, every time a member is moved to open up her or his personal boundaries, a new form of resistance may be expected. This is why the Intimacy crisis may last for longer than the Authority crisis. The Intimacy crisis resembles the blossoming of a tree. Only one or two buds open up at first. As the climate of the group warms up, more buds gradually join them until the whole group reaches the full blossom of the Mutuality phase. We may say that during the Intimacy crisis resistance to opening up boundaries is multi-focal.

Clarifying

Clarifying includes all the ways we identify links among bits and pieces of communication. In this sense, confrontation; that is, pointing out discrepancies in members' communication, is a form of clarifying. In the example, confrontation is used quite actively, as in entry 24, when Jane says to Joyce Cook: 'So, you do want John to tell Ruth off and when he does, you worry. Doesn't make sense, does it?', or when Clive (entry 42) confronts the group with their assumption that Betty Carr does not want to go 'too far' in her exploration. Another discrepancy is taken up by Jane (entry 52) when she asks Betty Carr herself if she feels under pressure.

Reaching for a feeling link is a clear form of clarifying connections among feelings, ideas, and behaviour. You can see Jane (entry 16) reaching for a feeling link when she asks Joyce: 'Do you remember? Did you feel angry or worried at what John had done?' Jane is even more direct just seconds after that (entry 20) when she says: 'I just wonder, Joyce, did you have any other feelings suddenly coming up?' Clive resorts to this type of intervention at a crucial point; when Betty Carr cannot decide whether to disclose her concerns. In entry 35, Clive simply says: 'Betty, there's something here that you recognise?'

Relating here-and-now to there-and-then can be seen in Jane's response to the discrepancy in Joyce Cook's expressions. In entry 24, Jane says to Joyce: 'Do you remember? Was there anybody else in your *own* life, maybe years ago, who had frightened you with shouting?'

Stabilising

Compared to the Authority crisis, stabilising is used more actively during the Intimacy crisis, particularly once at least one member breaks through an area of taboo. This relative increase in resorting to stabilising may have to do with the individualised nature of the emerging disclosures. As explained before, once group members realise that it is possible to share more personal concerns, they are driven in two contradictory directions. One direction is to join in and reveal their own personal concerns. The other direction is to hold back such disclosures. Usually members resist personal disclosure because they fear that their own personal circumstances are too different from those of others, and so no other person can understand them, not even in this group.

So, even after an initial breakthrough, members often put up new barriers to personal disclosures. The transition to fully sharing the personal level is blocked again. Yet, because the initial breakthrough is often experienced as liberating to the person concerned, often the residual resistance that arises later is less intense. Therefore, later on openness can be directly encouraged through small step-by-step responses that flow in the opposite direction of the low barriers. Such responses gently direct members towards a desired level of openness and, in this sense, these responses are forms of stabilising.

From entry 46, various forms of stabilising are evident. In entry 45, Betty Carr blocks further disclosure with a firm statement: 'Never mind'. You can see Jane counteracting this block by saying warmly (entry 46): 'I mind, Betty. What do you want to say? What about understanding?' Clive challenges a similar block when Betty Carr assumes that group members will not tolerate being 'confused' by her disclosure. In entry 56, Clive asks directly: 'What's so awful about us getting confused?'

Betty Carr seems just about ready to say more, and so Clive gently but directly encourages her to take a little leap in the desired direction, and so break the taboo. In entry 62, Clive simply says: 'You think you can say just a bit about what it actually was?' Yet, Betty's fears of group members' reactions about the disclosure still seem to linger. So, both Jane and Clive offer support in this area of taboo. In entry 66, Jane simply reassures Betty Carr that she 'can understand how painful it was for you'. Later on, while Betty Carr continues to deepen her exploration, Clive (entry 68) lends her a hand by saying: 'There was more to it?' Clive continues to show that he does understand by simply and reassuringly rephrasing Betty Carr's messages in entry 74: 'He had told her he was gay. Yet, they got married.' Clive offers even more direct support in this taboo area in entry 80: 'But at the time you could not possibly know that, could you?' Then Jane deepens the attempt to support Betty when being confused. In entry 82 Jane says to Betty: 'It's difficult for you to understand it even now, Betty?' Betty Carr's loneliness in struggling with confusing memories is then further stabilised by Clive who re-defines the issue as a group problem. In entry 84, Clive asks the members: 'How about the rest of the group? How difficult is it for us?'

Altogether, at first the Intimacy crisis calls for a great deal of Amplifying disturbing experiences. Clarifying the upheaval is vital. Stabilising is needed mainly later on to support communication in areas of taboo.

Further implications for practice

Turning points

Major turning points have been mentioned already, so it is necessary only to summarise these here. The first turning point occurred early on when, in entry 6, John Cook said: 'It's not that which I mind...' The workers could have taken John's reaction to mean that 'becoming a baddy' was a side issue, and could have pressed ahead with consolidating John's achievement in disciplining Ruth. Had they done so, the workers would have resorted to stabilising. Yet, as already explained, the workers sensed that more was involved and began to amplify John's deviation.

The second turning point was in entry 19, when Joyce Cook confirmed she was pleased with her husband 'pulling his weight'. The workers yet again, could have taken this to mean that no further work was needed. So, the workers could have stabilised the interactions by sharing in Joyce Cook's delight. Yet, these workers sensed that Joyce Cook was also struggling with 'unexpected' feelings; that is, with a deviation from being pleased. Therefore the workers began to amplify Joyce's disturbing feelings.

The last turning point occurred towards the end of this episode. The workers could have further deepened Betty Carr's explorations of the implications of her parents' relationship for her own relationship with her daughter. Yet, at that juncture the workers seemed more concerned to mobilise members' support of Betty Carr. So, in entry 84, the workers chose to re-define the issue as a group problem; 'How difficult is it for us?', briefly exploring whether members were ready to adopt new norms that supported such personal explorations.

Being aware of the levels involved seems to have helped the workers steer the group towards increasing the range of issues explored while also maintaining an adequate degree of peer support in doing so.

Sustaining polarities

As various polarities have been mentioned already, a summary may be sufficient here too. It may help remembering that *amplifying* is inevitably tied up with *stabilising*, and the *personal* level inevitably clashes with the *interpersonal*. Bearing in mind these ties can help practitioners steer through the Intimacy crisis. Practitioners may let the group go through a number of cycles: amplifying distressing experiences at some points and stabilising new relationships at others. These cycles may have to be repeated every time another member attempts to cross the boundaries into the personal level. Practitioners may also let the group fluctuate a number of times between the upheaval of unexpected *connectedness* at the personal level, and the safety of *separating* experiences through interpersonal roles. Anticipating such fluctuations between apparent opposites may help practitioners show the warm acceptance that members need for continuous therapeutic work.

The relevance of the Intimacy crisis

When group members break personal taboos, workers are often emotionally moved. Workers often tend to feel that 'we are really getting there now'. Indeed, the potential benefits of the Intimacy crisis have already been mentioned. Yet, problems may arise in practice when practitioners decide that all groups must go through this particular crisis to achieve their goals. Practitioners can unintentionally pressurise group members to reveal feelings the members do not consider appropriate in a particular group. The quality of learning that may result should be of concern to every worker.

A clear example where the Intimacy crisis does not appear to be appropriate can be found in the educational model described by O'Hara (1988). Preparing adults for the tasks of fostering, the model maintains the boundaries of the interpersonal level throughout the duration of the group.

The Intimacy crisis does not appear in the problem-solving model of Rose and Edleson (1987) either. While working with children and adolescents Rose and Edleson do describe behaviours that others may see in a different light. Examples of these are horseplay and giggling in the middle of a problem-solving discussion. Such behaviours are considered by the authors to be 'disruptive' (Rose and Edleson 1987, p.302). Faced with such a disruption the worker adopts 'a firm and well-articulated tone of voice with intense eye contact ... The group leader looks from person to person and physically moves towards the most disruptive member' (Rose and Edleson 1987, p.303).

However, dynamically inclined practitioners such as Brandler and Roman (1991) would say that the group leader who acts in this manner is suppressing the 'covert' messages that may lurk behind the giggling and the horseplay. Systemic thinkers would consider such disruptions to be deviations from the norm of the group, and that such deviations may have to be amplified if the youngsters are to be helped to share what really worries them most.

Clearly, the problem-solving model is not concerned with such hidden messages. Yet, many children and adolescents find it very difficult to share personal experiences with adults and with their peers. Some even get into trouble while struggling to contain and even to conceal their distress.

It is for each practitioner to decide whether or not groupwork with such youngsters should reach the personal level and, therefore, whether to enable the Intimacy crisis. The present framework can only offer tools with which to identify the difference between such an approach and, for example, the one adopted by Malekoff (1997).

Yet another stance can be seen in the personal growth model presented by Benson (1987). Following Benson's control stage, members have 'organised themselves in terms of responsibility and power ... They are ready to explore what it means to be emotionally involved with each other' (Benson 1987, p.123). Members are then seen to be gradually and comfortably moving into the 'affection stage' when very intimate experiences are shared. This smooth transition into the stage equivalent to the present Mutuality phase, is somewhat unusual. Benson's personal growth model does not include the Intimacy crisis either. Perhaps this crisis does occur but is not described. Equally, it is possible that 'because of the emergence of an interpersonal structure which is supportive of group activity and concerned to further the best interests of members, (Benson 1987, p.123), these members develop sufficient sense of freedom at the interpersonal level first. When members move toward the personal level, they may not feel so ambivalent, and so they may open up their personal boundaries more comfortably in such groups.

Moving as it often is, the Intimacy crisis does not seem to be universally needed. The present evolving framework may help practitioners identify the nature and dynamics of this crisis so they may facilitate it when this crisis clearly benefits group members.

When it erupts, the Intimacy crisis is often a prelude to the Mutuality phase.

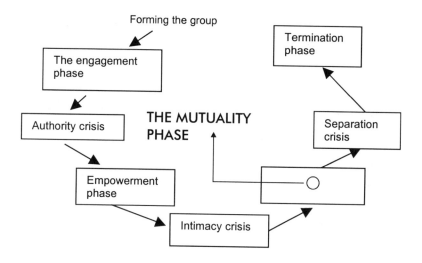

Figure 5.2 The Mutuality phase

Main features of this stage

Two of the paradoxes that arise during the Mutuality phase are:

> Regression: In order to progress you need to regress.

> Creativity: In order to create you need to destroy.

The Mutuality phase takes place at the heart of the personal level. During this phase clarifying is paramount, while amplifying is actively used to some extent, and stabilising is very sparingly employed.

The example

1. David Thomas: The point is, if we're honest, sometimes we do want something for *ourselves*; not for the kid, but for ourselves for a change.

2. Betty Carr: Yeah, as if that was a sin.

3. Jean Robinson: Exactly what? Which sin are you talking about?

4. Joyce Cook: I don't know, in general, there's a point when I feel; well, today to hell with it, I'm going to spoil myself.

5. John Cook: But you don't.

6. David Thomas: It's not a sin, is it? I just fancy, well, right now, I
   fancy a bit of a laugh, yeah some comic relief, like Clive and Jane;
   you give us a little panto show, I've got a title for you: how about
   'a day in the life of a social worker'? You can take the mickey, I
   don't mind.

7. Moira Morris: But I DO! What is this?

8. David Thomas: For Pete's sake Moira, give us a break, will you?

9. Jean Robinson: What is this between the two of you, huh?

10. Moira Morris: (terse) There's nothing between the two of us, I can
    assure you. (angrily) It's just that I did not come here for a childish
    mucking around.

11. David Thomas: (sarcastically) Oh dear, I'm so sorry, our lady of
    virtue.

12. Moira Morris: (irritated) No need to go sarcy, just because you can
    never take responsibility.

13. David Thomas: (raising his voice in protest) I can't what?

14. Moira Morris: You heard.

15. Gerald Robinson: Come on you two, we've been through this
    before.

16. David Thomas: I muck around? It's people like you, heavy, no-fun
    people, who turn children's lives to muck.

17. Moira Morris: (flatly reprimanding) David, I've had enough of this
    loose talk.

18. David Thomas: (pitched voice, cringes, face showing hurt) I'm just
    saying ...

19. Jane: David, what has happened? Something's changed, your voice.

20. David Thomas: Hum, I don't know. It's this tone of voice, it hurts
    my eardrums.

21. Jane: Moira's way of using her voice?

22. David Thomas: Weird this is. For a moment, just for a split second,
    I felt like a little kid again, being told off.

23. Clive: What I hope is that in this group adults who are already parents can also feel what it's like to be children.

24. David Thomas: Easily said ...

25. Clive: David, who else, perhaps when you were a child, used to tell you off like Moira? You get at her often. Does she remind you of anybody?

26. David Thomas: Well, a bit, my Mum perhaps ... always being serious, always demanding work, putting me down for larking around.

27. Clive: Your Mum put you down for being cheerful?

28. David Thomas: Not in words.

29. Jane: Yet, as Jean said, the two of you don't let go. It takes two to tango. Moira; any of your memories come up?

30. Moira Morris: Look, we ARE here to work, we have responsibilities for children.

31. Jean Robinson: (with urgency) Moira, did your Mum get stroppy?

32. Moira Morris: (detached) I'm not sure.

33. Jean Robinson: (pressing) But did she? Come on.

34. Moira Morris: (less involved) My Mum? I suppose ...

35. Jean Robinson: (impatiently) Yes, what DID she do?

36. Moira Morris: (indifferent) Tell you the truth, I don't remember.

37. Jean Robinson: (eagerly) Did she ever shout at him, or something?

38. Jane: Jean, you seem to ask a lot of questions that don't seem to get very far. You know, sometimes behind so many questions there is a statement just dying to come out. Try it Jean, if you could not ask any questions anymore, what statement, what opinion, or wish would replace them?

39. Jean Robinson: (surprised) Oh! Opinion? It's not a matter of opinion. It's experience.

40. Clive: Your experience, Jean?

41. Jean Robinson: Well.

42. Betty Carr: So, what was your experience?

43. Jean Robinson: It was ... You need to have been through this to understand.

44. Joyce Cook: Tell us, Jean, how was it for you?

45. Jean Robinson: Well, he never mucked around. No, he just sat there, not saying anything, TOTALLY useless. And the money ...

46. Clive: This was your Dad, I presume, not your son?

47. Jean Robinson: It was so hopeless. I used to think. Maybe, maybe if I understood him more I could help him. I used to ask him all the time, Mum did too, what's the matter Dad? What do you want to do?

48. Jane: Trying your utmost to get to the bottom of it.

49. Jean Robinson: Trying, but not succeeding.

50. Gerald Robinson: It's a bit strange this one. I know it was awful. The trouble is that some of it seems to linger. It's just occurred to me.

51. Clive: Some of the old habits seem to linger even now?

52. Gerald Robinson: Well, when Jimmy won't tell us what's the matter.

53. Jane: Jean, what do you do when Jimmy won't tell you?

54. Jean Robinson: Hum, well, I suppose so. Haven't realised. (reflecting in silence) (to Gerald Robinson) I do go on a bit, don't I? I'm just trying to make sure I understand him. I ask in order to understand.

55. Gerald Robinson: (with some sadness) I know you mean well.

56. David Thomas: (smiling) As Jane would say, I hear a 'but'. What's the but, Gerald?

57. Gerald Robinson: But it does not work. It makes things worse. Jimmy just gets stroppy and does something outrageous, and then ... you know...

58. David Thomas: It just gets worse.

59. Jane: You know Jean, thinking about it, even in this group, you have been asking questions far more often than you have expressed your feelings or ideas. I wonder, perhaps that's something you want to change.

60. Jean Robinson: It certainly doesn't work. If there's another way. If I can understand him without asking questions.

61. Clive: (to group members) Any suggestion?

62. David Thomas: I'd just tell him what I myself feel or think.

63. Betty Carr: It's OK for you, you're a man. Women are not supposed to ...

64. David Thomas: I've met a number who have never hesitated.

65. Jean Robinson: I'll probably hesitate but it's worth trying.

This example has to be incomplete, but you can probably see the exchanges meandering among members; each invisibly leading to the other. Such weaving of personal concerns into a tapestry of shared experience has to continue for a while, but we have to stop here to see the dilemmas contained in these contents.

Contents: Group themes and dilemmas

As explained in Chapter 2, during the Mutuality phase members closely connect with one another and in the process find out what separates them.

This phase probably resembles Tuckman and Jensen's (1977) stage of 'performing'.

You can see how one member readily sparks off reactions in the others in this example. There are also instances here when one member easily, naturally, and accurately communicates empathy to another: Betty Carr to David Thomas ('Yeah, as if that was a sin', entry 2), and David Thomas to Gerald Robinson ('It just gets worse', entry 58). Members also help one another by putting forward just the right question. Examples are when Betty Carr says to Jean Robinson very simply: 'So, what was your experience?' (entry 42), and when Joyce Cook follows the same line by saying to Jean Robinson: 'Tell us, Jean, how was it for you?' (entry 44). Notice also David Thomas' response to Gerald Robinson in entry 56. While being aware he is entering a worker's role ('As Jane would say'), David nevertheless offers a well tuned-in empathic enquiry, commenting: '... I hear a 'but'. What's the but, Gerald?'

Increased openness among members characterises the Mutuality phase. As members open up to one another they often begin to identify with each other quite strongly. Each senses the other's joy, apprehensions, pleasure, or hurt – sometimes even before these are fully expressed in words. It is as if a connecting thread emerges among the members. In psychodrama the term 'tele' is used to describe this reverberating experience. In group analysis, the more modest term 'resonance' is established: 'as if a certain tone or chord struck a certain specific resonance in the other receptive individual' (Foulkes 1969, p.290).

Such enabling resonance is often deeply nourishing. Members strongly feel the uniqueness of the experience and many immerse themselves in it. During the Mutuality phase, members feel warmly connected with others. Now they are safe in the knowledge that whatever they feel, someone in the group will respond appropriately; someone will resonate. Although not always consciously, such deep emotional care-taking often reminds members of being totally cared for in their early childhood.

Yet, the Mutuality phase is not all sweet and rosy. Those members who were not looked after very well during those days can be often moved to remember their deep yearning. Suddenly these members feel an intense need; one that they have not allowed themselves to feel for a long time. They just wish that somebody would take good care of them now.

In both cases, the Mutuality phase can easily have a regressive effect on the members. Quite a number of them may strongly feel the wish to return to early childhood, but not without a struggle. In our example, Jean Robinson bombards Moira Morris with questions (entries 31–37) that do not seem to help. On the face of it, Jean is pursuing the right course, but only on the surface. As the later exchanges suggest, Jean is actually erecting a barrier by using 'treatment talk' rather than asking herself some painful questions – ones that may lead her to explore her own memories of her own childhood.

Although not always desirable, sometimes it is helpful to go back to childhood years, when certain strategies of behaviour were learnt. The member concerned may then realise that presently disabling responses were right then, in the past, but they get in the way now in the present. Some conditions were there, when the member was a child, which led that member to adopt this particular behaviour, but by now these conditions do not prevail anymore. So, there is no point in continuing to adopt that original pattern of behaviour now. You can see the powers of regression in the example too: David Thomas seems to be pulled towards his childhood and wishes to 'lark around', while Jean Robinson is pushed to become the irritated and useless parent – a role similar to the one she had to act towards her own father. Both movements are grounded in the paradox of regression: in order to progress you need to regress (Smith and Berg 1987, pp.125–130).

Paradoxically, the value of regression for learning is in enabling a member to create emotional distance from a parent. Yet, it is often difficult to achieve such distance because the member is still emotionally attached to that parent.

You can see an example of this difficulty in Jean Robinson's case. Jean has to re-evaluate her present strategy of caring for her son. To do this, Jean will have to let go of bombarding her son with questions. Yet, bombarding questions is still connected, for Jean, with memories of caring for another focus of affection: her father. At this stage, bombarding a loved one with questions still has a special meaning for Jean. For her, this strategy still symbolises that she cares. Caring through bombarding questions has become part of Jean's sense of her own identity.

Therefore, at a more personal level, holding on to this often unconscious attachment to a parent, charges the person's sense of identity with meaningful past memories. To disentangle herself from the strategy of bombarding people with questions, Jean may have to distance herself from an unconscious emotional focus of that strategy: in her case, her father.

Quite often it is necessary to enable a member to create emotional distance from the parent who, earlier on, engendered the member's need to adopt a particular strategy.

To create this distance, a person like Jean Robinson has to amplify one feeling fully. Hard as it is, being angry has this positive function: through expressing anger we differentiate ourselves from the person to whom we are attached. When expressing anger we establish that we are different from that person.

This is probably why the initial thrust of such anger is often undifferentiated − it includes everything associated with the person with whom one is angry. So, to let go of her inquisitive manner, Jean Robinson has first to destroy her attachment to her father; in her words, to see him as '*totally useless*'. Indeed, this is the paradox of creativity: in order to create, one has to destroy (Smith and Berg 1987, pp.143–147).

Understanding the paradox of emotional creativity can help the workers realise that the Mutuality phase is not necessarily a period of lasting bliss of mutual support. If new relationships are to be created, anger, hurt, resentment, and destructiveness must be allowed too.

It may be possible to link these experiences also to Yalom's (1995, pp.69–105) curative factors. The whole range of factors under the heading Family Re-enactment appears relevant to the paradoxes mentioned here, for example: 'Being in the group was, in a sense, like being in a family, only this time a more accepting and understanding family'. Insight may also emerge out of these experiences; for example, through 'Learning that I react to some people or situations unrealistically (with feelings that somehow belong to earlier periods in my life)', and instillation of hope; as in 'Seeing that others had solved problems similar to mine', seems likely too.

This script does not offer quite a number of experiences, as well as facilitative responses, which occur during the Mutuality phase. Still, the major dynamics of resonance are probably demonstrated. Let us look at these now.

Choosing the appropriate level: The personal level

It is almost unnecessary to say that most of the experiences of the Mutuality phase are personal. Many connections are made and re-made so that differences among members can be sustained. Indeed, individual differences among members are not only allowed, but are virtually cherished as sources of learning. An example of this is when Jean Robinson is helped to see the similarities and the differences between her feelings towards her mother compared to Moira Morris' detachment from hers (entries 31–47). As already mentioned in Chapter 1, to enable such degree of openness, a very loose structure is needed with no clear centre.

The personal nature of the Mutuality phase means that the workers may wish to do their best to avoid blocking these freely flowing experiences, and so may refrain from taking a too directive stance. This is why many workers tend to limit their responses to moments where the process would not move forward without them. In this example too, the workers respond only when the members' responses to one another are repetitive, too confusing, or potentially disabling. Most of the time, the workers 'follow the flow' of experiences during this phase.

The Mutuality phase is at the heart of the Personal level.

Processes

Clarifying

During the Mutuality phase the workers usually take a more marginal position in the group, and very much focus on clarifying. In the example, you can see that the workers wait for quite a while until they respond. The first opportunity occurs only after the conflict between Moira Morris and David Thomas reaches a certain pitch. Jane (entry 19) then offers David Thomas a form of confrontation, saying: 'David, what has happened? Something's changed, your voice'. In saying this, Jane points out the discrepancy between David Thomas' argumentative words and his hurt voice. Jane continues by focusing on David Thomas' description of Moira's voice (entry 21). Clive then relates the here-and-now to there-and-then by suggesting to David (entry 25): 'Who else, perhaps when you were a child, used to tell you off like Moira?' David Thomas makes this connection quite easily, and all Clive has to do is to communicate empathy with him (entry 27): 'Your Mum put you down for being cheerful?'

The next clarification seems necessary when Jean Robinson repeatedly bombards Moira Morris with questions, while Moira Morris continuously detaches herself (entries 31–37). Jane (entry 38) then uses another form of mild confrontation, observing to Jean, 'you seem to ask a lot of questions that don't seem to get very far'. Jane continues by reaching for a feeling link when she asks Jean Robinson: 'What statement, what opinion, or wish would replace them (the questions)?' Jean Robinson seems to need some help in finding out, and so Clive enables her to own negative feelings by briefly commenting (entry 40): 'Your experience, Jean?'

Further exchanges seem to call for relating here-and-now to there-and-then from Clive, who suggests to Jean Robinson (entry 46): 'This was your Dad, I presume, not your son.' For a while, the workers then concentrate on communicating empathy as in entries 48 and 51, and then they take the opposite direction: connecting there-and-then to the here-and-now of Jean Robinson's behaviour in the group (entry 59). These are forms of clarifying too.

Amplifying

This example does not include the use of amplifying. Yet, my experience is that in similar groups a degree of amplifying may be necessary when some members struggle with certain personal experiences of which they are not entirely aware, and when members become ambivalent about sharing these concerns.

Stabilising

You can see that due to the nature of the Mutuality phase, the workers use stabilising rather sparingly. When David Thomas openly talks about feeling like a little kid again (entry 22), Clive uses the opportunity to verbalise the norm he hopes the group will follow. Clive says that he hopes that 'adults who are already parents can also feel what it's like to be children' (entry 23). In fact, Clive is approving of the paradox of regression. It is necessary to stabilise members' involvement again only towards the end. Clive then re-defines an issue; that of Jean Robinson finding another way of talking to her son, as a group problem. Clive (entry 61) simply asks other members: 'Any suggestion?', but Clive implies a desirable spread of participation by directing attention away from only one member and towards everybody else.

Altogether, the Mutuality phase seems to call for considerable emphasis on Clarifying. Amplifying may be needed to some extent, and Stabilising is usually sparingly used.

Further implications for practice

Focused as it is on personal experiences, the Mutuality phase tends to progress in subtle and often slow rhythms. Therefore, the present very brief comments can only touch on major points.

Turning points

During this brief episode, one turning point emerged. The conflict between David Thomas and Moira Morris had been festering during the previous stages. During the Mutuality phase that conflict surfaced fully between entries 7 and 30. Yet, just as Jane was trying to involve Moira Morris again, Jean Robinson took hold of the conversation, bombarding Moira Morris with questions. Faced with this apparent interruption, the workers had a choice: the workers could have asked Jean Robinson to wait for a while, and then direct attention back to Moira Morris. It can be seen that the workers did not choose to be so directive. As a result, one might be concerned whether Moira Morris was ever enabled to explore her rather stern approach to relationships.

My experience is that working within the Mutuality phase often raises such dilemmas. Had the workers directed attention back to Moira Morris, they would have assumed a directive role that might have re-defined the positions in the group. Such intervention could have made the workers more central, and the members more peripheral, and so might have restored the structure of the Empowerment phase. Yet, many workers, like Clive and Jane, are mindful of the need to loosen up boundaries during the Mutuality phase. Therefore, at this stage workers are often rather hesitant occupying too central a position.

When workers let go of the directive stance they sometimes worry about neglecting the needs of some members, such as those of Moira in the present example. Yet, such temporary neglect is not necessarily crucial. As explained before, since the Mutuality phase is so unstructured, members do not know exactly how to react, and so they fall back on their previously established patterns again and again. Members repeat certain patterns of behaviour because at some level they are attached to these patterns – they feel that these patterns are 'natural' to them. Acting 'naturally', members tend to resort to the same patterns – often without being aware that they do so. As one of my earliest supervisors used to say: 'If it's important it *will* return'. As long as the group is kept unstructured repetitive patterns, such as the one adopted by Moira Morris, are likely to come up again and again during this phase. Therefore, the workers can safely wait for a person like Moira to repeat such a pattern later on. Then, when Moira's pattern does return, the workers may be able to address Moira's needs without usurping a central position.

Sustaining polarities

At source, *stabilising* and *amplifying* are reciprocally bound to each other. Indeed, the *interpersonal* and the *personal* levels are similarly entwined. Appreciating these paradoxical dynamics may help practitioners pace their responses during the *Mutuality* phase.

Experience suggests that members fluctuate between greater and lesser degrees of openness during this phase. At times members amplify their personal distress, but then they retreat to stabilising expressions with more interpersonal and even social concerns. Openness rarely progresses linearly; more often it evolves in cycles. Each approach of moving towards greater personal openness alternates with a retreat – with periods dedicated to consolidating the new learning interpersonally. Such cycles seem to enable learning. The retreats from the personal level allow members to apply each new experience to their relationships with other members of the group, and to their relationships outside the group too. Practitioners can accept that change tends to fluctuate through these polarities, and so, they may accommodate their responses accordingly.

Relevance of the Mutuality phase

In some models of group development the various equivalents to the Mutuality phase are seen as 'the work of the group'. This view of personal concerns as the only 'real business' can be seen in Tuckman and Jensen's (1977) label of 'performing', as well as in Corey's (1995, pp.110–123) term 'Working stage'. Even Brammer, Abrego and Shostrom (1993), whose framework does not necessarily lead to this conclusion, still seem to hold on to the same view. When these authors write about the 'Affection stage' they add that: 'This stage is considered the 'working' stage of a group' (Brammer, Abrego and Shostrom 1993, p.243). The implication is that unless the group reaches this stage, no 'work' is done.

It is quite difficult to see personal explorations as *the only* focus of every group when very different types of groupwork are considered.

In some groups the equivalent experiences of the Mutuality phase are evident and clearly related to the purpose of the group. An example can be found in personal growth groups described by Benson (1987). The period called by Benson 'the Affection stage' does resemble the Mutuality phase. As Benson put it: 'Now the members are beginning to explore the opportunities and potential for involvement and *interdependence* and require from the worker an approach that permits and enhances group functioning on its own behalf.' (Benson 1987, p.128) Yet, such groups are only part of the full range of groupwork.

The educational model for foster parents (O'Hara 1988) does not seem to need a clear Mutuality phase. Indeed, none of the experiences described seems to resemble spontaneous mutual resonance among members implied by this phase.

The same seems to hold for the problem-solving model applied to adolescents (Rose and Edleson 1987): no clear Mutuality phase seems to be included in this model either. It can be argued that such loose structure as required for the Mutuality phase may be too threatening for children and adolescents. However, other practitioners may disagree with this statement.

In general, it is not obvious that all groups must focus on personal concerns and thereby go through the Mutuality phase. This phase appears to be relevant to groups whose goals clearly include a focus on the exploration of intimate individual experiences. Such a focus may not be the only one, and so there is no reason to accept that other stages are less beneficial to members of these groups.

By elucidating the dynamics of the Mutuality phase, the present framework may enable practitioners to clarify their choice. Practitioners can clarify why they emphasise this phase in some groups, and why they relegate it to the background while working with others.

In all time-limited groups the impending end is usually known in advance. Even so, some groups are gripped by a certain crisis before they end. This *separation crisis* will be discussed next.

CHAPTER 6

Separation Crisis and the Termination Phase

Two stages will be demonstrated in this chapter: the Separation crisis and the Termination phase.

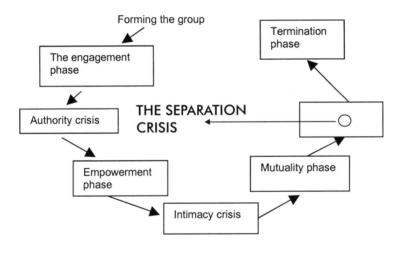

Figure 6.1 The Separation crisis

Main features of this stage

The paradox of courage may arise during the Separation crisis as members realise that to see hope they have also to accept despair. During this crisis the group detaches itself from the personal level and transforms its boundaries to encompass a wider area of the interpersonal level. Amplifying disturbing experience is paramount, clarifying is often associated with amplifying, and stabilising is relatively moderate.

The example

1. Joyce Cook: I've been thinking ... I know it's a long way away, what – five months? But if we plan, why not do something nice together for Christmas?

2. David Thomas: We certainly deserve it, we've worked hard enough.

3. Betty Carr: Shall we have a meal out?

4. Moira Morris: Well, perhaps each can bring a dish.

5. Jean Robinson: (to Jane) Can we have a meal here then?

6. Jane: We want to have something nice for ourselves in here. Feels good to me. I also wonder how this may be connected to what we said last week.

7. John Cook: Last week?

(long silence)

8. Assiff Khan: Excuse me, I forgot to say, I'll have to leave earlier tonight.

(long silence)

9. Clive: Leaving in the middle is sometimes easier and sometimes more difficult.

10. Jean Robinson: You're getting at something, but it escapes me, Clive.

11. Clive: Well, last week we remembered that it was five weeks to go. Then this group will end, we'll be leaving this group.

(long silence) (Assiff is now very busily sorting out the pockets in his jacket, emptying some, replacing contents in another, looking at his watch, staring at the window)

12. Jane: Assiff, something is keeping you very busy suddenly.

13. Assiff Khan: Me? Oh, sorry, I think I lost that note.

14. Jane: You lost ...

15. Assiff Khan: That note, you know ...

16. Jane: We are all going to lose something, unless of course a Messiah is born to change it for us.

(Assiff Khan withdraws into his chair, arms folded, looking at his knees)

17. Moira Morris: Ha, ha, very funny, Jane.

18. Jane: It's not really, is it?

19. Assiff Khan: It is not funny at all.

20. Gerald Robinson: Assiff, I don't remember seeing you as worried as you look now.

21. Clive: Quite a number of people look worried to me, and that makes sense. I hope we can all talk about it.

22. Betty Carr: Five weeks!

23. Assiff Khan: (to Clive) It's all right for you – not much of a difference.

24. Clive: Are you saying, Assiff, that it will make a great difference to you?

25. Assiff Khan: (face becomes very serious) Well ...

(tense and long silence)

26. Jean Robinson: It's a bit cold in here, isn't it?

(Assiff looks very tense by now and close to tears)

27. Gerald Robinson: (warmly) I'm worried about Assiff. Something's going on which he is not talking about.

28. Jane: Assiff, you think you can find the words? (Assiff Khan shakes his head, saying 'no')

29. Jane: Sometimes it's so difficult to find the words. Sometimes it's better to just show people what we feel. Assiff, perhaps you can show us, with your hands?

(Assiff Khan opens both hands and lets them drop to his sides)

30. Clive: Two hands that say more than a thousand words. (pause)

31. Jane: Assiff is helping us get in touch. What do his hands say to each of you?

32. Gerald Robinson: Empty. Empty hands.

33. Betty Carr: Bare, nothing.

34. David Thomas: No help.

(Jean Robinson chokes on a sobbing sound)

35. Joyce Cook: Alone.

36. Moira Morris: Deserted.

(Tears appear now to run down Assiff's face)

37. Jane: It's difficult this end, painful, even frightening. (pause) Perhaps it's even more so for Assiff right now.

38. Assiff Khan: It's that feeling, no man's land...

39. Moira Morris: But you are in this land, you are staying in Britain, aren't you?

40. Assiff Khan: I know. That's what it may seem to you.

41. Clive: But not really for you, Assiff.

42. Assiff Khan: Well, me – I am different.

43. Clive: You are the only Asian member?

44. Assiff Khan: It's different. It's the first time (chokes again).

45. Gerald Robinson: This group has been a first time for you.

46. Assiff Khan: I'm all right with Asian people, but for the first time...

47. Jane: This is not an Asian group, yet...

48. Assiff Khan: It's a group. It's a place where I felt all right...

49. Jane: It's not an Asian group yet you were all right being part of it.

50. Assiff Khan: Jasmin is like that. That's the problem. She does not feel totally Indian anymore and she certainly isn't white. With her Mum not really speaking English very well, it's so confusing ...

51. Betty Carr: Sort of no man's land?

52. Assiff Khan: How will I help her now? I can't talk to Asian people, they don't understand the white ways. I can't talk to white people, they don't know our ways. I'm left with nothing.

53. Clive: Not being white and not totally Indian anymore, nothing is left?

54. Assiff Khan: This group just showed it all to me. It's made me feel it more. So now?

55. Jane: It's as if, suddenly, there's nowhere to go from here.

(heavy silence)

56. Assiff Khan: It's back to square one.

(silence)

57. Gerald Robinson: Seems like nothing is left. Back to the old problems ...

58. Assiff Khan: There'll have to be something. I can't go back to THAT!

59. Jane: We can't go back to those problems and we can't stay as a group, so ...

60. David Thomas: It's frightening. Last night I felt like hitting him again. I haven't for so long, but suddenly ...

61. Jane: Suddenly it all came back, David? You felt like hitting Mike again. But what did you actually do?

62. David Thomas: Oh, I remembered; as we said, whom am I angry with: him or me? Myself, for not getting something for myself. So I cooled it.

63. Clive: That's great, David! That's the real difference. Now you have other ways of dealing with not getting something for yourself.

64. Betty Carr: If there was SOMETHING. Something to take with us.

65. Clive: Let's find out. We've been through so much, surely ...

66. Moira Morris: I haven't realised how much this group has meant to Assiff. Well, it's meant a lot to me too. I have learnt to let go of my bossy side, to have more fun with the kids. It's really going well now.

67. Jane: Perhaps we can go round, sort of take stock of how it's been.

68. Joyce Cook: Funny, I don't mind John being angry now; it's gone. So now he tells Ruth off, oh – quite often.

69. John Cook: (smiling) I've become the good baddie.

(members relay memories of funny episodes, difficult moments, helpful experiences etc.)

The Separation crisis surprises many workers, but it has its own sense that can be seen in the emerging themes and the dilemmas.

Contents: Group themes and dilemmas

This episode begins with the members planning a Christmas meal to occur at a time when the group will not meet anymore. On the face of it, planning a Christmas meal after the group is going to end does not make sense. Instead of dealing with the end, the group seems to choose the unrealistic task of planning a meal for a time when it will not be together. The group appears to be getting away from the reality of it coming to an end. In systems terms, such a flight of fancy is a 'deviation' from the range of topics that is expected at this point of the group's work. The workers are very conscious of this digression. Yet, obvious as these are, the workers' direct attempts to address this deviation (entries 6 and 11) do not seem to achieve any result.

On the contrary, the process escalates, and soon the members communicate two discrepant messages. One message is concerned with the Christmas meal. Planning this meal now implies that there is still plenty of time ahead. The other message is conveyed by Assiff Khan, who is short of time and has to leave. The group is *polarised* by two messages: one is that time is unlimited and the group can plan a meal regardless of the time left. The other message, represented by Assiff Khan, is that there is no time at all. Assiff is not able to stay even for the present whole session. The discrepancy suggests to the workers that, as a whole, the group is *ambivalent* about exploring the end of their work together.

Following Brandler and Roman (1991, pp.164–190) it is often worth noting that at least one of the opposing messages has two layers: the 'manifest' and the 'latent'. The manifest contents are clear – what you hear is what you get. The latent contents are often ambiguous and hard to comprehend at first, as these comprise layers of message – one enclosed within the other. What you hear also signals another message that the person may be hesitant to express overtly.

In this example the layers are communicated by Assiff Khan. The manifest contents are expressed in his words: forgetting to say that he has to leave earlier (entry 8). The latent contents are first expressed through Assiff's bodily gestures – Assiff is looking for the note he lost (entry 13).

For relationships to be meaningful the latent contents have to be made manifest too, so that all feelings are shared by all. This is why it is often necessary to reach out to the latent contents. Special efforts are often needed to clarify the latent contents because these are often communicated in a symbolic fashion. Accessing these latent contents can be helped by realising that some contents appear in disguise. Some expressions contain cues to a precious treasure left in most unexpected places. Latent contents are often wrapped up in symbols. Buried inside the symbols as they are, the latent contents are not dead – Assiff is clearly still pre-occupied with the relevant issues. Latent contents are simply masked by symbolic expressions. Faced with these, the worker has to help members unwrap certain messages so that their inner contents can be heard.

You can see how such unwrapping is pursued by Jane. In the example, Jane first points out the bodily signs of the latent contents. She says: 'Assiff, something is keeping you very busy suddenly' (entry 12), but Assiff Khan is still responding in a symbolised fashion; referring to a lost note (entry 13). Jane then begins to refer to this message as a symbol – the lost note may symbolise losing the group. In small steps, Jane and later Clive then try to enable the members to acknowledge the symbolic latent contents in words; that is, make the latent contents manifest (entries 8–19).

Slowly and very painfully the hidden messages surface fully. The short time left (entry 22), and the coldness which will remain when the group ends (entry 26), come up first. Then, with even greater poignancy, more is expressed: the feelings of leaving empty handed, of feeling bare, of getting no help, and of being so alone and deserted (entries 32–36). These feelings can be particularly acute for a minority of one, like Assiff Khan, but are often experienced by all members who share the ending of an enabling group. At the core of this crisis is an intense feeling of *despair*. As Assiff Khan says: 'It's back to square one' (entry 56), and Gerald Robinson echoes: 'Seems like nothing is left.' (entry 57). Once the reality of ending sinks in, acute grief, fear, and sadness may flood the group and a sense of emptiness and helplessness may prevail. The members may even invalidate any gain they have made during the life of the group, as Assiff Khan does in entry 54 by saying: 'This group showed it all to me. It's made me feel it more. So now?' The workers are likely to be subjected to intense pressure from members to save them from this predicament.

Indeed, fear and despair may prompt members to remember initial problems. David Thomas experiences this so-called 're-capitulation', in entry 60, when he refers to suddenly feeling that he may hit his son again. Such surfacing of previous problems is one of the most difficult aspects of this crisis. Faced with such a risk, workers can lose heart too and decide to extend the group. Yet, in such circumstances, prolonging the group's life is likely to be a mistake. In spite of the prevailing feelings, the re-capitulation of problems is usually not a full return to the initial problematic situation.

Coping with such re-capitulation, workers may be helped when they bear in mind that before any sense of hope arises, the members may have to be allowed to experience and express fully the despair they feel about ending the group. You have probably noticed that the workers do not interfere with any reassurance or advice until entry 65. The workers first let the members share their fears, sadness, and despair from entry 20 throughout the agonising exchanges that culminate in entry 62.

Sustaining such troubled times with the group can be assisted by realising the nature of the paradox involved. Smith and Berg (1987, pp.147–151) called it 'the paradox of courage': to see hope you have to accept despair.

Often it is necessary to enable the group to accept despair very fully. Painful as it is, fully despairing of the possibility that the group will continue, is necessary. Only after members reach the bottom of despair do they themselves begin to rise in a search for hope.

You can see how Assiff Khan goes through despair and then surfaces with a call for hope: 'There'll have to be something' (entry 58). Once the search for hope begins, the workers can elicit more signs of hopefulness from other members. In entry 61 Jane draws out David Thomas. Jane first acknowledges the return of old problematic feelings: 'Suddenly it all came back, David? You felt like hitting Mike again.' Then Jane encourages David to test the new and promising reality: 'But what did you actually do?'

Of course, it is then helpful to reinforce good news. In the example, news of success is brought by David Thomas: the return of his worries ('feeling like') was not accompanied by the return of disabling behaviour (actually hitting the boy). As Clive (entry 63) says: 'That's great, David! That's the real difference. Now you have other ways of dealing with not getting something for yourself'. Other members are encouraged to identify their own growing strengths too (entries 64–69).

In the process and without necessarily noticing this, the group seems to merge the two previously incongruent polarities. Members come to accept as true that there is no time anymore; there is no time for continuing with the group as it is. Now members also realise that, in another sense, there is more time, but the time they do have is for recognising and further developing their strengths, as some begin to do in entries 66–69.

Group members have to struggle in this way with the paradox of courage so they may give up the group and form other relationships outside it. Yet, the struggle itself may be beneficial to them too. At least two of Yalom's (1995, pp.69–105) curative factors may surface during the Separation crisis. Existential factors, such as 'Recognizing that no matter how close I get to other people, I must still face life alone', and 'Learning that I must take ultimate responsibility for the way I live my life no matter how much guidance and support I get from others' are probably clear examples. As this crisis is resolved, *instillation* of hope may feature too; for example, the experience of 'Seeing others getting better was inspiring to me'.

The Separation crisis can threaten workers' sense of competence and derail them from enabling the group to move on. Therefore, it may be helpful to bear in mind the overall direction that may help the group, and this can be found by adding the other two aspects of the dynamic.

Choosing the appropriate level: From the personal to the interpersonal level

The flight of fancy into planning the Christmas meal at the beginning (entries 1–5), can be interpreted as the members' attempt to overlook the need to change the boundaries of their involvement.

Yet, the workers are aware of the price of such a denial. During the Mutuality phase the group has been involved at the personal level. Yet, now the boundaries of the personal level do not seem to serve the new needs. Faced with the denial of the impending end, the workers accept that they will have to help the group move out of the personal level. This the workers do by amplifying the distressing signals that come from Assiff Khan. Indeed, as the Separation crisis erupts members' level of involvement shifts too.

Now it turns out that Assiff Khan is worried about social concerns: being of Asian origin in a white society (entry 46), and an interpersonal one; that of being a father (entry 50). David Thomas too is concerned about his way of being a father (entry 60). The Separation crisis directs members back to the social level and to their interpersonal roles; in this example, of being fathers.

Returning to the interpersonal sub-system is necessary. At this stage the members have to end the group and cope with their daily life differently. Therefore, they have to detach themselves from membership in this group and increasingly focus their attention on external relationships. Out there are prescribed roles, such as being fathers, with which members plan to cope differently now. To do so, members have to begin to translate what they have learned at the personal level to strategies of coping with social concerns.

In the example, you can see how Assiff Khan begins this transition. In entry 42 Assiff states a social issue bluntly: 'Well, me – I am different'. Assiff then expands on his social concern when he talks about his daughter who 'does not feel totally Indian anymore and she certainly isn't white' (entry 50). Then, in entry 52, Assiff Khan starts to search for the ways he may now assume the role of being an Indian father in a white society. Clearly, complex issues are involved and so – a person like Assiff Khan will have to explore more interpersonal issues if he is to find answers.

In spite of being tempted to extend the exploration of personal issues, most of the time workers may help members more by enabling them to detach themselves from the personal level and move towards the interpersonal one. Of course this transition is never easy. As pointed out, polarising attitudes and despair are often inevitable during this crisis. Earlier, during the Intimacy crisis, the workers helped members move from the interpersonal to the personal level. Now they have to help members move in the opposite direction: to the interpersonal level. In both cases, the shift is hard because two sub-systems are involved at the same time: the personal and the social. Indeed, the crisis is where the two overlap; at the interface between the levels. The transition to the interpersonal level involves members in re-structuring their relationships – from those appropriate inside a group to relationships that will help them outside. Such re-structuring is necessary if members are to form themselves into a network of mutual aid.

During the Separation crisis the group detaches itself from the Personal level and re-defines its boundaries to include more issues at the Interpersonal one.

Processes

Amplifying

As already mentioned, the workers first try to stabilise interactions. In entry 11, Clive simply notes: 'Last week we remembered that it was five weeks to go'. Yet, this stabilising response has no clear effect. This is why the workers then concentrate on amplifying one polarity of the systemic deviation. This polarity is conveyed by Assiff Khan when he sorts out the contents in his pockets.

Amplifying begins in entry 12, when Jane draws attention to Assiff Khan's bodily gestures, saying: 'Assiff, something is keeping you very busy suddenly'. As Assiff Khan still responds symbolically, Jane amplifies the only contents associated with the latent distress. Jane (entry 14) merely says. 'You lost …'. Yet, this is not enough – Assiff Khan is still expressing himself only symbolically. So, Jane tries humour as a form of amplifying. Jane (entry 16) suggests that: 'We are all going to lose something, unless of course a Messiah is born to change it for us …'

Sometimes warmly humorous comments can be helpful. Humour strikes two chords at the same time. Resorting to humour, it is often better to begin with overt contents as these are visible to all. In the example, the two chords are the two overt yet polarised messages. One message is that there is still plenty of time till Christmas. The other message that time has been lost. Through the temporary confusion created by humour these two chords are struck together, and so – everybody can hear the discrepancy between them more clearly.

It can be seen that Jane's humorous comment does have a helpful effect. Although Moira Morris (entry 17) protests, and Jane has to retract somewhat, now Assiff Khan really begins to talk (entry 19), acknowledging that it is 'not funny at all'.

Yet, members still find sharing the full distress difficult. Clive (entry 24) has to communicate empathy with Assiff Khan, but it is left to Jane (entry 29) to really help Assiff find the words through an experiential growth game. Jane invites Assiff Khan to show what he feels inside by making overt and exaggerated bodily gestures. The members are then brought in to express their reading of Assiff Khan's gestures and thereby amplify them (entries 31–36).

Indeed, sometimes growth games can be used to amplify disturbing experiences. These games are not forms of amusement. Rather, these are sensitive interventions that enable members to safely accentuate bodily gestures that convey members' covert distress (Manor and Dumbleton 1993).

Still, even this amplification may not be enough. Up to now, members have expressed interpersonal aspects of being in the group. Now it is clear that Assiff Khan is also struggling with a social fear; as he says (entry 42): 'Well, me – I am different'. You can see Clive (entry 43), then Jane (entries 47 and 49), and then Clive again (entry 53) – each reaching out to Assiff. Each worker communicates empathy with Assiff Khan's struggle to find his own way as an Asian in a white British society.

Of course Assiff Khan is not the only member who finds the separation difficult, and the workers involve the rest of the members by communicating empathy with each member (entries 55, 59, and 61). These responses lead to the covert contents, of fear and despair, being shared by all members.

Clarifying

Possibly thrown by the initial talk about a Christmas meal, the workers first try to clarify the message. Jane (entry 6) begins by communicating empathy: 'We want to have something nice for ourselves in here'. This instance of clarifying does not seem to lead to a realistic focus, probably because it is mixed with a form of stabilising; that is, questioning the connection of what members say to the discussions during the previous week. Therefore, the workers change their approach. During the rest of the session the workers indirectly attach clarifying messages to their amplifying responses. The workers keep communicating empathy with members – particularly with Assiff Khan's struggle. While doing so, the workers' empathic responses contain also cues to new links. An example is when Jane responds briefly in entry 14: 'You lost …': her empathic yet ambiguous response also highlights the possible link to losing more than a note; perhaps losing the group? Likewise, Jane's humorous comment in entry 16, embraces a hint, as most humorous notes do, to an unseen link which may be discovered. Clarifying is offered here indirectly – as a prompt rather than a full explanation.

Such indirect forms of clarifying are not always sufficient, and their present use probably reflects the workers' preference. These workers try to facilitate members' own work of assimilating the experiences in their own ways. In other groups, clarifying may be offered more directly, but in both cases it seems important to see to it that the experiences are increasingly meaningful to members. Whatever the means to this end, members should be actively involved in clarifying this crisis.

Stabilising

Unlike some crises, the present one begins with the workers actually trying to see if stabilising interactions may be experienced as helpful by the members. As mentioned before, in entry 6, Jane offers a mild form of confrontation; pointing to the discrepancy in members' conversations, by saying: 'I also wonder how this may be connected to what we said last week'. As there is no clear response to Jane, Clive tries the same message more explicitly, when in entry 11 he says: 'Well, last week we remembered that it was five weeks to go …'. Yet, none of the members seem to take this up as a directly stabilising message either. So, the workers turned to amplifying the distressing experiences instead.

During the rest of this episode, stabilising is offered for further reasons. In entry 21, Clive re-defines the issue of a member being worried – turning this into a group problem by saying: 'Quite a number of people look worried to me, and that makes sense …'. This is a form of stabilising as Clive has a definable range of exchanges in his mind. Clive steers the members towards more equal participation. In entry 61, Jane helps David Thomas recognise the new solution he has found while handling his son, and in entry 63, Clive voices David Thomas' achievement in doing so. Both of these responses are aimed at consolidating David's new and desirable level of employing parenting skills.

Indeed, towards the end, Clive (entry 65) proposes larger group goals when he says: 'Let's find out, we've been through so much, surely …', and Jane extends this larger goal into action in entry 67, by virtually suggesting: 'Perhaps we can go round, sort of take stock of how it's been'. Such interventions are designed to direct members' attention to a range of behaviours the workers consider desirable, and so these workers' responses constitute forms of stabilising too. Yet, compared to the use of amplifying, stabilising is offered rather moderately during this crisis.

Altogether: during the Separation crisis Amplifying is paramount, Clarifying is actively contained in it, and Stabilising is relatively moderate.

Further implications for practice

Turning points

Perhaps the major turning point in this example was when Clive (entry 9) commented about Assiff Khan's wish to leave early: 'Leaving in the middle is sometimes easier and sometimes more difficult'. Jean Robinson's response (entry 10) suggested that Clive struck a chord – he was 'getting at something' that was real. Indeed, Clive was alluding to the reality of group members' ambivalence about exploring the end of the group. A choice emerges: to return members to the relevant issue or to enable a crisis.

It is not always helpful to assume that members are ambivalent. It is probably more effective to test out this possibility by first attempting a stabilising response to a deviation, as Jane and Clive did in entries 6 and 11. Only when group members' reactions to direct stabilising do not make sense, do the workers have reasons to surmise that the members are ambivalent about the way ahead. Then a turning point has to be faced – ambivalence among members is the signal for the need to amplify messages and for undergoing the turmoil of a crisis that often follows.

Another turning point arose in this example around entries 28 and 29. Suddenly it became clear that Assiff Khan, who up to now had come across as highly articulate, was not able to find the words to express his distress. At that point Jane could have given up on Assiff Khan and could have considered him incapable of expressing his feelings. Yet, Jane decided to simply try a different route; by-passing words for a while. This is the advantage of the present evolving framework. As long as the dynamics, in this case around Assiff Khan, are clear – various techniques may be employed. In the present example, the turning point involved leaving the use of words and resorting to the non-verbal technique of a growth game.

Sustaining polarities

Bearing in mind that, at base, *amplifying* and *stabilising* are tied to one another may prevent practitioners from forcing Separation crises onto groups. While it seems very important to enable groups to work through the Separation crisis, imposing such a crisis does not stand to reason. Thus, rather than quickly starting to amplify every deviation, practitioners can always begin by offering simply to stabilise interactions, as the workers did in this example. If group members are not ambivalent about approaching the end of their group, they are likely to accept such an intervention, and comfortably explore what they need to do now that the group is about to end.

However, if the group members are ambivalent about exploring the end, one or two of them will probably begin to amplify the deviation themselves. In the example, Assiff Khan fulfilled this function for the group. In response to the workers' stabilising, Assiff became engaged in activities that appeared overtly even more divorced from the reality of the group; that is, emptying his pockets and looking for a lost note. Workers who are in tune with the reciprocal tie between stabilising and amplifying may wait just for that; for a message that is overtly even more deviant. It is likely that behind this overt deviation there lies a covert one; a fear that nobody in the group dares to articulate. In the example, the fear was that of being abandoned when the group would come to its end.

Another polarity is between the *personal* and the *interpersonal* levels. The Separation crisis may evoke many fears in group members. If, for quite a while, members have been closely connected at the personal level, workers may lose sight of members' need to separate at the interpersonal level. Yet, as this example shows, members must find separate interpersonal solutions if they are to cope at the social level in which they are contained. This need may be acute for a person like Assiff Khan, who is a minority of one. Such a person may then need the workers' help, in translating aspects of the social level into separate interpersonal solutions. Personal politics become pertinent at this stage.

Relevance of the Separation crisis

Much has been written about the importance of enabling group members to thoroughly work through separation issues before the group ends. Of the examples discussed here, the personal growth model (Benson 1987) is the one that shows this crisis fully. Benson calls this period 'the Ending stage', and notes that the group appears to suffer 'a psychic shock' as members are faced with the full impact of 'separation issues' (Benson 1987, pp.146–148).

Yet, even the Separation crisis does not appear to be universal. Neither the educational model (O'Hara 1988) nor the problem-solving model (Rose and Edleson 1987) include clear references to these experiences. Perhaps this is as it should be. Not all groups are set up to enable members to experience ambivalent feelings related to deep attachment. Such ambivalence is central to intimate relationships but learning about intimacy may not be identified as a major goal in certain groups. In addition, the more structured the group the less such ambivalence is likely to arise.

When members are not ambivalent about the ending of the group and/or the group is highly structured, members are less likely to experience Benson's 'psychic shock'. Foster parents may even feel pleased that they completed the programme satisfactorily and prepare themselves to celebrate their achievements. Children and adolescents in problem-solving structured groups may simply acknowledge their regret, and move on to terminating the group. The present evolving approach to group stages can account for such differences too.

Whether they go through a *separation crisis* or not, all time-limited groups have to work out how to end. This is the subject of the last section of this part.

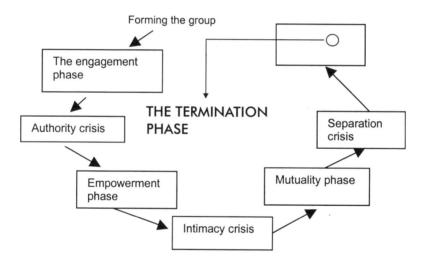

Figure 6.2 The Termination phase

Main feature of this stage

The Termination phase gives rise to the paradox of dependency: for any party to be independent it has to depend on the arrangement as a whole. Some personal concerns arise during this phase, but members mainly elaborate the interpersonal level while making clear references to the social level.

During the Termination phase stabilising is paramount, clarifying is actively used, and amplifying is hardly evident.

The example

1. David Thomas: Last week I felt we were losing ground, it was all slipping away.

2. Assiff Khan: It's this togetherness and honesty with people. So different.

3. Jane: I'll miss this unusual feeling too, it's been giving me so many examples of living together, living with the differences ...

4. Clive: We don't have to lose everything. Let's continue: what has each of us learnt, what can each of us take with us now?

5. Joyce Cook: I think I learnt to let John know what frightens me, so it does not get in the way of taking care of the kids. I am certainly going to try and continue like this; (smiles) saves so much energy...

6. Jean Robinson: I think I learnt to say what I think instead of asking questions all the time. I think I'll stick with that.

7. Gerald Robinson: I hope you will!

(each member identifies what they have learnt which they wish to take with them for the future)

8. Jane: It's good to hear so many positive plans. But, you see, what we also know is that after a while some people drop the new ways. It's a sad thing, but many do. Unless ... Well, unless they plan for this in advance. It seems so important, to think ahead – who will help me stick to the new ways and exactly what they should do about it. Let's do this now, let's plan. For example, Jean – shall we start? If you find yourself bombarding Jimmy with questions again, what will help you regain the ground? What will help you telling him instead what you feel or think?

9. Jean Robinson: Yeah, I'm quite worried about this. I suppose Jimmy will sulk again, then do something silly. Then I go mad. Terrible really.

10. Jane: So, what may help you reverse course again, as you have done?

11. Jean Robinson: With me it's a bit of a problem. Remember? It was like this here too. Until I saw Moira going quiet as I questioned her, I did not realise what I was doing.

12. Jane: So, you are one of those people, I am sure you are not the only one, who needs to see the consequences of their behaviour before they consider changing it.

13. Jean Robinson: Well, how else will I know? I don't stand there in front of the mirror all the time.

14. Jane: Of course not. So, how will you see the signs and remember them early enough, before Jimmy does something silly and you go mad?

15. Jean: I suppose, one way, is to make rules for myself.

16. Jane: For example?

17. Jean Robinson: (laughing) Robinson rule number one: If he sulks I stop, not go on.

18. Gerald Robinson: Sounds good to me. Robinson rule number two?

19. Jean Robinson: Robinson rule number two: Once he sulks I stop and go out of the room. Then think: what do I feel, or want, or think.

20. Jane: Makes sense to me, but why go out of the room?

21. Jean Robinson: That's how I am. I can't find out with other people around me.

22. Gerald Robinson: Not even me?

23. Jean Robinson: I'm afraid so. It's nothing against you, but I need to be alone. Besides, if I go out maybe you come in, ha? We agreed that you too should now talk with Jimmy about feelings – not only fishing and football.

24. Gerald Robinson: Yeah, OK, we did agree. I need more practice I suppose, but the deal stands.

25. Jane: As we said, part of the planning includes Gerald. You can't change it all on your own. He must do some things too. How will each of you know that you are on the right course? What will encourage you in this?

26. Gerald Robinson: I suppose, if there are no problems. If there aren't then it's fine.

27. Clive: May I butt in? You see, this is what many people do. They wait for a problem to come up. They don't keep an eye on things,

but just wait. It's like an invitation – 'you problem, you catch me, then I'll deal with you'. So, all the time they are worried: when will the problem catch up with them? The more worried they are the more they may make mistakes. So, the problem will turn up. Self-fulfilling prophecy we call this. But there is another way. I wonder, if, for at least half a year, until the new behaviour really becomes a sort of habit, I wonder if you would like to try to keep a sort of diary. Every week, let's say on Sunday afternoon or whatever, you two meet together, open the diary and begin to write in it. But, as you write things down you also discuss them. Let's call this 'a writing conversation'. In the writing conversation each of you tells the other of the good things you saw the other doing. Concentrate on those bits you have just talked about. Gerald to listen and talk to Jimmy about feelings. Jean to say what she feels and thinks instead of asking questions. How about that? How about this talking diary?

28. Gerald Robinson: I'm game. Half a year sounds manageable.

29. Jean Robinson: (teasingly) Will this mean not talking in between? (in a determined voice) OK, yes, let's go for it.

(change maintenance and generalisation plans are worked out with each of the members)

30. Gerald Robinson: I remember, Assiff, you saying that the end of the group leaves you in limbo, no man's land, with Jasmin in particular.

31. Assiff Khan: Yes, well ...

32. Clive: Surely it's not only Assiff who will be a bit lost.

33. Betty Carr: No, the truth is that you lot know Sammy much better than many now, from what I've told you ... and you know me, with my little quirks. Who else will understand?

34. Moira Morris: Well, none of us is going away.

35. David Thomas: I've been thinking, there's the telephone. If people don't mind ...

36. Jane: Perhaps you can phone each other when in a tight corner?

37. Jean Robinson: (excited) Well, this time I'm not going to ask ABOUT telephone numbers. I'm going to ask FOR them!

38. Betty Carr joined by others: Well done Jean! What a nice change!

39. Jean Robinson: I AM going to ask and to say. I would like to have others' numbers. My number is: come on, paper out, pencils ready, my number is xxxx xx xxxx. Any offers?

(members exchange telephone numbers)

40. Jane: This is one of the things I appreciate most. People offering to help one another when the group ends.

41. Clive: And what happened to our Christmas meal?

42. Moira Morris: (teasingly) We won't be here for Christmas, you forgot?

43. Clive: Not for Christmas.

44. Betty Carr: But there can be a meal.

45. Assiff Khan: Do people like some Indian dishes?

46. Gerald Robinson: Go well with grilled fish, have you tried?

47. Moira Morris: Beat fish and chips. I think fruit salad will top it.

48. Clive: Are we saying we will have a meal together, as a goodbye? I'd like that.

49. Joyce Cook: (in jest) I'm sorry, by name I should be, but I'm not much of a cook. Still, I'm game. Something will have to turn up.

(practical details worked out and agreed)

All's well that ends well? Let us see the emerging themes and dilemmas.

Contents: Group themes and dilemmas

Tuckman and Jensen (1977) seem to recognise this phase as 'adjourning'. Levine (1979, p.247) briefly mentions that even after the Separation crisis is over, members may still feel some hostility about the end of the group. Levine sees members as struggling with the dilemma of expressing hostility versus feeling guilty about feeling hostile.

Indeed, the Separation crisis may not be resolved in one session. You can see it lingering into the beginning of this example too. David Thomas says: 'Last week I felt we were losing ground, it was all slipping away' (entry 1), as if the new ground is still slipping away now. Sometimes further working through the separation is needed. In this particular example the group seems to move comfortably forward when Clive (entry 4) offers a lead: 'Let's continue: what has each of us learnt ...'. Indeed, during entries 5–8, members begin to take stock of their learning and identify the changes that they want to maintain.

Yet, good intentions are not enough. To update John Donne: no man or woman is an island. It is foolhardy to assume that everybody can sustain change on his or her own. There may be exceptions, but sooner or later, most people succumb to the pressures of their physical, social, and interpersonal environments. Behaviours that are praised and rewarded continue, and those that are ignored, reprimanded, or punished tend to cease. Change takes place within such transactions.

Because of the transactional nature of change, it is helpful to plan ahead to the time when group support will not be available. Such planning is suggested by Jane (entry 8). Jane urges each member to make contingency plans to a time when change 'slips away'. Such forward thinking usually includes rehearsing the worst script; as if the previous problems are bound to reappear. This form of rehearsing relapse can immunise members against losing heart later on, if the problems do recur. Members may well need such immunisation.

The reason is that during the initial period following the end of the group, members often tend to revert back to their previous disabling behaviours; a phenomenon known in family work too (Manor 1984, pp.114–121). While rehearsing relapse, it is important to include in the plan those people who influence members' behaviour. You can see Jean Robinson involving her husband in sustaining the changes she wants (entry 23), and how she is supported in this by Jane ('You can't change it all on your own', entry 25).

Even when sustaining change is well planned, it may still fail. When this happens, it is often not the plan which is faulty, but its monitoring and reinforcement. Clive gives a little lecturette about this in entry 27; warning the members against simply waiting for problems to arise, and encouraging a pro-active approach. The pro-active approach to sustaining change means that some behaviours are continuously monitored by the parties themselves, and praise is offered to the person able to keep up the new habits. Clive suggests the 'writing conversation' as an aide. The Robinsons can set aside time to review their own behaviours. They can talk as they write the diary and express appreciation of each other's efforts to maintain their respective changes. Devices such as this 'talking diary' may in themselves generate constructive exchanges. Both parties, of husband and wife, may then draw strengths from the emerging experiences while they continue to purse their respective goals.

More generally, peer interdependence; the mutual dependence that members can form among themselves, can be sustained also in the form of a social network of mutual aid. The example shows a network emerging during entries 30 to 39 – members begin to exchange telephone numbers and include in the network their 'minority of one': Assiff Khan.

As a network of mutual aid emerges, it needs to be fostered and nourished. One way of nourishing the future network is by creating a symbol of the transition towards it. The symbol can be something the group does together at the end which members can remember as a sign of their interdependence.

Generated at that point, such a ritual can become a symbol that cherishes commitment and inspires each member in her or his relationships with the others later on. This is why Clive takes the initiative towards the end and, while teasing the members warmly, raises the idea of a shared meal (entry 41). A shared meal has to be co-ordinated, and co-ordinating a meal can remind members that each can sustain her or his independence only if each accepts some degree of dependence on the arrangement as a whole.

All these strategies are underpinned by another paradox. Smith and Berg (1987 pp.139–143) called this 'the paradox of dependency': 'For any part of a system to be able to act independently, it must accept its dependency on the other parts with which it together makes up a whole.' (Smith and Berg 1987, p.140). In a group, members may find their ways of coping with a relapse more easily when their strategies also involve others. Of course, these strategies have to include the influences and participation of other people with whom they have relationships in their daily lives.

Altogether, monitoring and maintaining change is a transaction too: each person can increase her or his independence when, to some extent, that person can rely on others' participation in the plan.

Such overall considerations are guided by the need to take an overview of the group's experiences as a whole. As discussed in Chapter 2, members and workers reach such a view by emphasising the basic communication mode of *completing*. The emphasis on the completing mode enables them to refer to experiences that have separated them from one another, as well as those that have connected them with each other. Out of these, members can then choose for themselves the experiences that will enable them to help one another in the future.

In itself, this struggle with the paradox of dependency may benefit members. When Yalom's (1995, pp.69–105) curative factors are considered, a number of these seem to be related to the experiences of this phase. Examples are: altruism; as in 'Helping others has given me more self-respect', as well as interpersonal learning as output; for example, 'Improving my skills in getting along with people', and some form of guidance; as in 'Group members suggesting or advising something for me to do'.

Many are the paths to such interdependence. This is why eliciting the full dynamics may help in seeing what they have in common.

Choosing the appropriate level: The interpersonal and the social

The episode actually begins with brief reference to the social level of 'togetherness and honesty with people' (entry 2), but following Clive's prompt, members share personal benefits they have gained through participating in the group. Joyce Cook (entry 5) is not frightened of her husband's shouting anymore, and Jean Robinson (entry 6) has 'learnt to say what I think instead of asking questions all the time'. Jane (entry 8) then encourages the members to reflect on applying these personal achievements to their roles as parents. So, members focus on their own ways of dealing with their children in the future.

Between entries 9 and 29, Jean Robinson and later also her husband, Gerald, explore strategies they can adopt as parents towards their son, Jimmy. You will note that now the Robinsons do not revert back to merely personal issues; those which distinguish them as separate individuals. Instead, the couple focus more on their individual ways of being parents; that is, on their interpersonal roles.

In entry 30, Gerald Robinson appears to revert back to the personal level by focusing on the particular situation that applies to Assiff Khan. Gerald's intention is probably supportive, yet Clive (entry 32) does not encourage this re-emergence of the personal level now. Instead, Clive raises a social concern, by commenting: 'Surely it's not only Assiff who will be lost'. The members take up this cue – most likely because they realise that they need to evolve a social system that will take the place of this group in the future. In entry 35, David Thomas suggests such a social arrangement: keeping in touch by talking on the telephone, and this is supported by Jane (entries 36 and 40). Clive (entry 41) goes even further by entertaining the possibility of a social event – the shared meal. It can be seen that after brief references to the personal level in entries 1–7, the group spends a great deal of time at the interpersonal level, as is evident between entries 9 and 34. From entry 35, the group is involved at the social level.

Altogether, the Termination phase may begin at the Personal level, but it will soon focus on the Interpersonal level, with clear references to the Social level being encouraged.

Processes

Stabilising

Most of the workers' responses during this phase are forms of stabilising; that is, steering interactions towards a desired range. You can see how Jane voices group achievements at the very beginning of the session. In entry 3, Jane comments on the 'examples of living together, living with differences ...' as indicating such a desired range. Clive follows this immediately (entry 4) with an attempt to elicit outcomes; that is, identify expected results of the group's experiences, when he says: 'Let's continue: what has each of us learnt, what can each of us take with us now?'

As members respond positively to this suggestion, Jane can then move on to elicit plans for the future. In entry 8 Jane urges the members to: 'think ahead – who will help me stick to the new ways and exactly what they should do about it'. Ideas for the future are emerging among the members now, so Jane articulates them by focusing on strategies of maintaining change. Jane helps Jean Robinson work out the details of these strategies in entries 10, 12, 14, and 16.

For change to be maintained, it has also to be extended to members' significant relationships. So, in entry 25 Jane helps Jean Robinson involve her husband Gerald. Yet, the Robinsons are only one example – other members can also adopt principles of maintaining change beneficially. This is why Clive (entry 27) virtually offers a mini-lecture which directs members towards being pro-active in devising strategies that help monitor achievements, and so generalise change in the future.

This thrust; to expand change to wider areas, is then pursued by Clive further. In entry 32, Clive says: 'Surely it's not only Assiff who will be lost'. By saying this, Clive re-defines Gerald Robinson's genuine yet personal concern for Assiff Khan, as a group problem, and Jane elaborates on the details when she works towards expanding a members' network by telephone in entry 36: 'Perhaps you can phone each other when in a tight corner?' Jane then reinforces the achievement in entry 40. It is left to Clive (entries 41 and 48) to prompt members to plan a social ritual; the joint meal, which may symbolise the joint direction they intend to pursue in the future. All these responses revolve around clearly identifiable targets: stabilising interactions towards the desired goals.

Clarifying

As in previous stages, clarifying, the linking of experiences to one another, is actively pursued during the Termination phase, but now clarifying is offered to expand the meaning of stabilising relationships – towards maintaining and generalising change, and towards the emerging network of mutual aid. Clarifying comments are attached to stabilising interventions when Jane (entry 8) points out that: 'after a while some people drop the new ways. It's a sad thing, but many do'. Jane also focuses on clarifying in entry 12, when she helps Jean Robinson see that Jean is 'one of those people ... who needs to see the consequences of their behaviour before they consider changing it'. Jane helps explore another link in entry 20, when she asks Jean Robinson: 'Why go out of the room?' It is Clive who expands clarifying when he talks about creating 'self-fulfilling prophecies' and the need to avert them, in entry 27.

Amplifying

By now you are probably aware that no clear indications of amplifying disturbing experiences can be seen in this example. With the Separation crisis resolved, members usually concentrate on termination issues. If the Separation crisis is assimilated, termination issues are not likely to be charged with ambivalence anymore. Therefore, it is rarely necessary to amplify experiences during the Termination phase.

> Altogether, during the Termination phase Stabilising is paramount. Clarifying is actively offered, and Amplifying disturbing experiences is hardly evident.

Further implications for practice

Turning points

Two turning points are demonstrated in this episode, and each is at the interface between two levels. The episode begins at the personal level between entries 1 and 7. The workers could have enabled the members to focus only on these personal achievements. Yet, you can see that these workers do not do so. The reason for the workers' choice has been explained before. These personal celebrations of achievements have their own value, but may remain confined to members' behaviour in the group or to only specific domestic situations. The long term value of members' achievements is in generalising them to more and more external situations. This is why Jane (entry 8) begins to direct members to the future rather than continue to focus only on the present. By encouraging members to 'think ahead', Jane sets the scene for exploring interpersonal arrangements. Jane's choice is driven by her understanding that few personal patterns can be sustained in the future without complementary interpersonal arrangements that support them.

Considerable amount of time is then spent at this interpersonal level where valuable strategies for maintaining and generalising change between the parents are worked out. Such interpersonal arrangements can be considered sufficient and left with the parents to survive the test of reality later on. Yet, the workers do not believe that the interpersonal level on its own is firm enough. They seem to hold the view that even interpersonal arrangements are vulnerable to pressure from larger social forces. Interpersonal arrangements can be eroded when they are not contained within a larger social framework.

So, when the opportunity arises in entry 35, Jane reinforces a collective social arrangement – that of creating the telephone network. In the same vein, Clive encourages a social ritual – the shared meal that is also a choice that nourishes social support among the members.

The workers' choices at each point reflect their conviction that relationships develop and grow through fluctuating among all three levels: the *personal*, the *interpersonal*, and the *social*.

Sustaining polarities

During the Termination phase, the main polarity is structural; that is, between the *personal* and the *interpersonal* levels. Appreciating that at source these two levels are reciprocally tied to one another, may help the workers. Although this is not demonstrated here, the workers can draw on this knowledge to steer group members towards a future network that accommodates both. Such a network will have its own rules and so will be contained by its own *social* level. That level will prevail beyond the differences among the members. At the same time, these very rules can be formed so that individual connections are sustained through separate interpersonal arrangements. Each member will then have to say how to be approached for help and what help that member may be expected to offer.

A pluralistic culture may be fostered; one that unifies members while at the same time encouraging them to validate differences among themselves.

Wider social concerns may then be included. Developing a mutual aid system that meets the needs of a minority of one; Assiff Khan, is a good example. The norms of such a network may include agreeing how Assiff Khan may share his particular social struggle of being Asian in a white society, how his family can be helped over language barriers, and how their particular culture may enrich the emerging network.

Relevance of the Termination phase

It goes almost without saying that the Termination phase is highly relevant to all time-limited groups. Although quite different from one another, the three examples discussed in the previous chapters all include a period at the end when termination issues are the focus. In all the examples you will find increased orientation towards interpersonal and social concerns that will arise outside the group.

The educational model (O'Hara 1988) dedicates the last of the six sessions to looking at support systems available to foster parents. Although parenting skills are still mentioned and the love that foster children need are recognised, most of the issues concern the parents' expectations for the future and the systems that exist around them meeting these expectations (O'Hara 1988, pp.53–54).

Within the problem-solving model (Rose and Edleson 1987) the experiences of termination are conveyed under the term 'generalisation'. These workers are very keen to ensure that the youngsters generalise the group experiences to their daily life. Therefore, adults who occupy significant roles in the youngster's lives are invited to the group towards the end. During these open sessions the members talk with these adults about their experiences in the group, and the help each needs to generalise and maintain changes outside it (Rose and Edleson 1987, pp.325–341).

The personal growth model (Benson 1987) does not make a formal distinction between separation and termination. By now you are probably aware that not all groups end in the same way, but Benson merges separation and termination into one when he writes about 'ending' (Benson 1987, pp.146–155). Still, careful reading of this account suggests that the author is aware of the difference. After discussing the 'ambivalent behaviours and feelings' related to separation, Benson has a separate section entitled 'Working with the group at termination'. He explains that during this time 'Members' interest and investment in the group is beginning to wane and your main job is to emphasise movement away from the group and towards other groups, members' own community, or workplace'. (Benson 1987, pp.148–149). Perhaps this account could have been more coherent if the difference between phases and crises was made clearer.

The Termination phase is likely to be needed whenever workers try to help members generalise in-session achievements to their outside life. So, in all such groups, time spent on the Termination phase is time spent very well indeed.

Finally, towards an inclusive view

With the Termination phase, the inclusive blueprint comes to its end. Major details of this blueprint have been suggested, but these have been offered only as examples to show how this framework may be relevant to practice.

The framework enables each practitioner to identify certain details such as turning points and inevitable tensions that have to be sustained for group relationships to develop. Yet, before these aspects are examined workers have to clarify for themselves which stages are likely to be most relevant to the group with which they work. What can be learnt about choosing stages from the discussion so far?

Even within this limited space it could be seen that the stages of the personal growth model fitted with the inclusive blueprint, almost *unchanged*. All the stages were identified apart from the Intimacy crisis. The personal growth model is depicted in Figure 6.3.

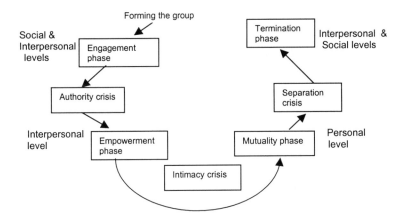

Figure 6.3 Personal growth model in relation to the inclusive blueprint

In contrast, the educational model borrowed, from the inclusive blueprint, only *three* out of the eight stages: Forming the group, the Engagement phase, and the Termination phase, as shown in Figure 6.4.

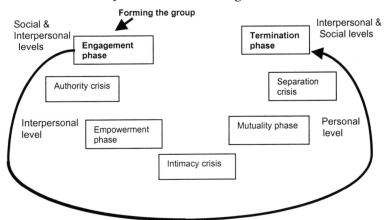

Figure 6.4 Educational model in relation to the inclusive blueprint

In between was the problem-solving model that drew on *four* out of the eight stages: Forming the group, the Engagement phase, the Empowerment phase, and the Termination phase. This choice is depicted in Figure 6.5.

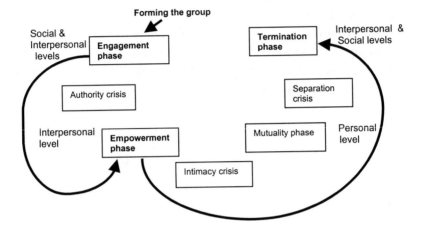

Figure 6.5 Problem-solving model in relation to the inclusive blueprint

The framework also facilitated questioning existing practice; for example, why the problem-solving model did not include the Intimacy crisis.

In addition, the inclusive stance can be used also to chart the likely stages of groups that have not been analysed within the inclusive blueprint yet. An example is a group for bereaved older adults. I am no expert in this area but I have had some practice experience. Even with such limited knowledge, it is possible to begin by drawing on two relevant sources: groupwork with older adults (Toseland 1990) and the literature on bereavement (Parkes 1986; Walters 1996; Worden 1983; Stroebe 1992–3).

Bearing these sources of knowledge in mind, it is probably safe to suggest that groups for bereaved older adults are similar to all others in one respect. In these groups too, efforts will have to be made to form each group properly, to engage it supportively, and to enable the group to end constructively. Within the inclusive framework this means that the groups will develop through the initial stage of Forming the Group, move on to the Engagement phase, and consolidate their work during the Termination phase. So far so very obvious. The vital question is what may happen *in the middle*.

Self-esteem and respect are obviously as important to older adults as they are to all other people. Yet, in itself – being respected is not the same as exercising power over others. Some people are, at times, quite content about their self-worth, without telling others what to do. There is enough knowledge to suggest that when older adults are bereaved, they are not likely to be so concerned about exercising power over others as they are about the confusing experiences of bereavement itself.

If that is true, then bereaved older adults may not be very concerned with the Authority crisis and the Empowerment phase. This may be so since these two stages are concerned with the direct use of power over other people. Bereaved older adults may not consider such issues to be of paramount importance at this particular stage of their lives. The frightening experiences of imagining that they are seeing the deceased alive and even imagining the deceased talking to them may burden bereaved older adults far more. These aspects of the bereavement process are common, but also very confusing.

In addition, other family members and the public at large usually see such common fantasies as 'strange' and even 'abnormal'. Therefore, like other bereaved people, older adults may need help in opening up discussion about their fear of 'going mad' and the meaning of these fantasies. In a group, these people can be allowed to approach such personal experiences safely. The problem is that an aura of taboo surrounds the sharing of these bewildering experiences in our society. Therefore, members of a bereavement group often have to enter the Intimacy crisis when permission to share individual experiences is gained.

Yet, the process of bereavement includes further hurdles. Longing for the deceased and the memories of intimacy shared with that person may be very intense. Such needs are very personal, and may turn the Mutuality phase into a very central experience for many members of such a group.

Further on, the loneliness experienced without the deceased may surface most powerfully. A sense of isolation may be particularly acute for older adults, as in our society it is often very difficult for older adults to make new friends. This is why the impending end of the group may exacerbate members' sense of loneliness. When this is the case, the Separation crisis may be particularly intense in groups for bereaved older adults.

However, when this crisis is worked through, the Termination phase may be a constructive stage, particularly when building new networks of mutual aid among the members is emphasised.

Altogether, I would suggest that a group for bereaved older adults is likely to develop through only *six* out of the eight possible stages: Forming the Group, the Engagement phase, the Intimacy crisis, the Mutuality phase, the Separation crisis, and the Termination phase. Such development may well be cyclical when certain stages will be repeated before the group moves on to new ones. Yet, such a group may not be very involved in the Authority crisis and the Empowerment phase. Schematically, the basic design for such groups will be as in Figure 6.6.

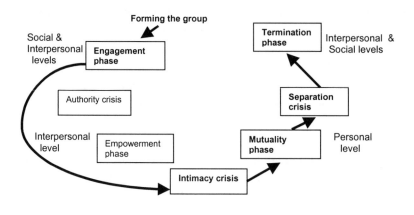

Figure 6.6 Basic design for a group for bereaved older adults

This discussion is just an example of the nature of the evolving approach to group stages. The detailed analysis of responses to the contents, the structure and the process; that is, to the dynamics, has occupied a great portion of Part 2. Such understanding of each stage may enable the worker to maximise the benefits related to experiencing that stage.

Yet more is involved – the inclusive stance avoids the attempts to impose on workers ready-made frameworks. Instead, workers are encouraged to uphold all the possibilities in mind while selecting from these the ones that are likely to meet the needs of each particular group. Furthermore, some workers may well emphasise different aspects of each of the three ingredients of group dynamics: contents, structure and process, during various stages. For example, the Mutuality phase may be helpfully experienced also at the interpersonal level rather than only at the personal one. Combining the ingredients differently will lead to new dynamics. In a manner of speaking, new stories may well continue to evolve in groupwork all the time. Yet, each new story will be equally comprehensible to those who combine the ingredients in other ways as the language of all the stories will be the same.

Indeed, telling different stories in the same language is the main aim of the inclusive stance.

Overall, reflecting upon these various aspects can help each worker anticipate some of the major experiences with which members may need help. Such prior reflection may also help each worker evaluate the group experience in relation to other groups, where some stages are the same and other stages are different.

It is quite likely that the added clarity will enhance the competence of each practitioner and improve the quality of groupwork as an area of practice. These advantages may lead practitioners to more fully appreciate the powers of paradox, and these are addressed as part of the following chapter on wider implications.

CHAPTER 7

Wider Implications
The Powers of Paradox

Concrete and formal ideas were explored in Part 2. This final section turns to more general reflections about paradoxes – the lynchpins of the inclusive stance.

By now, you probably have developed the inclusive habit of pitching ideas against one another. You probably realise that at one point *contents, processes,* and *levels* were *separated* from one another, but then these aspects were woven together into *stages*. Stages were separated into *phases* and *crises* but then also *connected* to one another to explain how basic designs were created. Some groups were described in terms of only very few stages yet it was argued that knowing all the stages of group development was necessary. Separating and connecting and then connecting and separating again: these cycles have meandered through the previous chapters.

What was the method and what good could come out of adopting it? The present final brief comments will address these questions.

The method itself is really quite simple. The world of group relationships is a web of continuously changing messages bouncing back and forth among the members of the group. Some of these messages are direct and obvious, others are vague and even hidden, and many are confusing. So, we try to find out what is going on.

Nothing is unusual about this position. People always ask themselves this simple question: What is going on? Yet, when you work with a group you ask yourself what is going on with respect to some aspects more than others. The method adopted here is to pay special attention to messages that appear at first contradictory; for example, structuring the group as opposed to letting the process flow, or *stabilising* in contrast to *amplifying*. Of course contradictory messages are not the only ones that can be heard in the group – many other messages are exchanged among members. Neither is focusing on apparent contradictions always necessary or helpful. Such a focus does not always arise naturally either.

This lack of concern about being so-called 'natural' is crucial. I always refer people who worry about being natural to the story about Marie Stopes. It is said that when this pioneer of family planning was going about persuading people to use contraception, she often encountered the argument: 'It is not natural'. 'Neither is brushing your teeth' was her reply. Being so-called natural is often a disguise for sticking with habits that do not necessarily help the group.

The groupwork discussed in this book is far more concerned with being intentional than with firming up existing habits. It is your intention to focus on some aspects more than others which makes you a groupworker rather than a person who spends time with a group. Focusing on apparent contradictions is simply one way of finding out a great deal about what is going on in the group.

Some apparent contradictions were made central in this book. One of these was the apparent contradiction between *process* and *structure*. By now you may be aware that processes are often seen as the opposite of structure. Yet, no group can sustain a pure process for very long. The slightest repetition of a fraction of a process; even the same direction of eye contact, leads to a pattern that in turn leads to forming a structure. Equally, no group can be totally structured. After a while, a totally structured group is likely to suffocate the members who are then likely to express boredom and resentment – quite spontaneously. When the members express themselves in this way the worker is caught by surprise, and thus – the worker becomes more spontaneous too. Lo and behold, before any intention is realised, processes are mobilised. Indeed, a close look at each of these opposites suggests that these two polarities also lead to one another. As was explained, one cannot be fully understood without referring to the other.

A far more helpful question is how to respond to such inevitable opposites. During the previous chapters, only few of the inevitable opposites were suggested, and the main pair arose out of the tension between process and structure. When opposites surfaced, the search began for a third aspect. That third aspect was not always obvious or even immediately identifiable. Yet, it was always assumed that a third perspective was hidden somewhere. Although not instantly recognisable, another focus was expected to lurk in the background – motivating people to shuttle between the opposites. It was also assumed that when we unearthed that hidden aspect, the inevitable opposites would appear not as contradictory but as complementing each other.

That third aspect was found by paying further attention to the contents of members' conversations, and these conversations tended to reveal an underlying *dilemma*. Once the contents revealed an underlying dilemma, process and structure were not seen as contradictory but as inevitable opposites – tied to one another by this third aspect which contained both.

Two inevitable opposites that are tied to one another by a third, often hidden, dimension form the structure of *'a paradox'*.

The inclusive stance was grounded in one such paradox, and that paradox was called 'the paradox of talk'. Yet, the focus on the paradox of talk was not chosen for its own sake. Surely, working with groups is not a playground for intellectuals chasing after paradoxes. There should be more immediate benefits for such a search. Indeed, the benefits arise out of another ability. The value of unearthing paradoxes is reaped when we learn to draw parallels. At various points, experiences that appeared first to be rather confusing were then clarified by identifying the ways in which these were parallel to one central paradox; the paradox of talk. You may remember that process, structure and contents were tied to one another in a paradoxical relationship. The most extensive example concerned the basic pattern of the inclusive blueprint of group stages. By showing that the inclusive blueprint was made of aspects that were parallel to the paradox of talk, the order of group stages was explained.

If the value of working with paradoxes lies in learning to draw parallels among phenomena, perhaps it is worth knowing a little more about the very act of finding such parallels.

When you reflect on the relevance of parallels a little further, you will probably realise that you have always known about them. We all discover parallels quite early on during our childhood. Lest you forgot, let me remind you of one game.

Paradox: A childhood play?

You may remember, I certainly do, how during childhood one game was particularly amusing. You can try it again now:

> Put your right hand on your tummy, and move this hand around in circles, stroking your tummy gently and pleasantly. Most children enjoy this. Now, put your left hand on the top of your head and tap it: up and down, and up and down. Slightly bizarre, is it not?

> Well, here is the game:

Now do both at the same time: with your right hand stroke your tummy in circles and, at the same time, tap the top of your head with your left hand.

Children who play this game often begin to laugh heartily. I remember how amusing I found this 'trick'. What is so funny about it?

From psychodynamics we know that laughter often releases tension, as an unexpected perspective is discovered. What do children discover? Some adults imagine that children just 'mess around' when they play. Perhaps it was Winnicott more than anybody else who showed that this was not so. A long time ago, Winnicott (1971) showed that while children played they were busy with aspects of the play that reminded them of their daily struggles: with their own development and with the adults around them. While playing, children use their intuition to draw parallels between various features of their play and certain aspects of their reality. None more so than when they keep demanding to hear the same old story – again and again. The figures of fairy tales, such as the famous ones by Hans Christian Andersen, are saturated with features that remind the child of her or his predicament: the ugly duckling, the heroic prince and many more. While listening to the tale, children work out the parallels between these figures and people that matter to them. Indeed, when adults do not provide these figures children invent them as they do in many improvised make-believe games. The meaning of children's play is in the details. If we go back to the stroking–tapping game we can see some important parallels.

In this game, the stroking right hand gives the child a soothing containing and connected experience as it moves in circles around the tummy. Such a continuous movement is likely to be parallel to the child's experience of spontaneous activities, nourishing hug, and any other relationship that flows uninterrupted and in tune with the child's own sense of the present.

The left hand is very different. Tapping the head sends separate pulses down the child's spine, and can be irritating. This tapping can easily remind the child of other interruptions: suddenly the child knows that it has to stop playing and go to eat; unexpectedly the child realises that the parent is busy with someone else; out of the blue the child hears the parent's rebuff of the child's behaviour. All these are discontinuous perturbations with which every child has to learn to cope.

During the stroking–tapping game the child experiences two contrasting messages: stroking is connected and soothing while tapping is almost unnerving with its separated pulses. Yet, the child is laughing. Why? Perhaps because the child realises: 'Hey, I can do it myself! I can engage two opposites to work *with* one another. Magic – isn't it?'

In this stroking–tapping game the child suddenly realises that she can conjure up a fascinating possibility. The child pays attention to each hand separately while, at the same time, she also focuses on the RELATIONSHIP between the two. The child is amazed: as if a third hand is at work. This third hand; the power of awareness to engage opposites, surprises the child and, in this sense, it is funny.

By engaging opposites, the child completes the picture and gives it added meaning. Now the game is still that of moving each hand, and yet, this very same game has gained an added edge. Now this is also an adventure in co-ordinating the movement between the two very different hands. It is likely that the child intuitively senses the parallels: a possible resolution of her/his main concern is at hand. Now she/he can accept that both continuity and sudden change are part of living and there may be ways of reconciling these opposites with one another.

So much for fun and games. Workers are not children, but perhaps we can all venture out to discover the benefits of sustaining paradoxical positions. While writing this book I have become aware of a number of advantages. Here are some of my observations.

Advantages of staying with a paradox
ARTICULATING STAGES

Understanding stages of group development can provide workers with signposts – markers of possible experiences that are likely to be crucial for group members. Yet, often the various aspects that define the stages are not very clearly described. Often there is a tendency to focus on some aspects of the stages at the expense of others.

The seminal work of Rogers (1970) on encounter groups is an example of focusing only on processes. Vital as processes are, when we exclude other aspects we may narrow the impact of groupwork considerably. The problem is this: an exclusive focus on processes does not alert the worker to the ways people outside the group are organised to exercise power over group members and how these structural arrangements prevent members from changing. The use and abuse of power is not captured very well when spontaneous processes are the *only* focus of attention.

The opposite tendency can be seen in the work of Donigian and Malnati (1997). The 'triadic model' proposed by these authors accounts for the relationship among the members, the relationships between members and the worker, and the relationships formed by the group as a whole. These structural aspects are very important. It can be shown that a great deal of influence; particularly in relation to exercising power, flows through these levels. Yet, when it comes to more intimate experiences something is missing here. The moment-to-moment exchanges, the non-verbal cues and whether these are congruent with the words members use – none are captured by identifying *only* the structural levels involved.

A third solution is to focus only on the contents of members' conversations. An example of such a choice can be found in the work of Doel and Sawdon (1999a). Helpful as it is in other respects, this approach too focuses on only one aspect of group dynamics. Of course, the themes that arise in the group are crucially important as these reveal members' immediate concerns as well as 'covert' – undeclared issues that trouble them. Yet, paying attention only to contents can leave workers unprepared to respond to some of the members' more complex needs. What people talk about is always relevant, but the ways they talk about each topic can be even more telling.

Are members just going through the motions of talking about oppression or are they investing their own feelings in the subject and trying to introduce change? The processes involved usually provide the necessary clues.

The structure within which the contents are explored matters too. Is this latest interruption just a sign of disrespect or is it a message that the group is about to enter a crisis in preparation for a new and more personal level of exploration? Understanding structural aspects of group development can help workers make a more informed judgement about such turning points.

The inclusive stance is different from all the previous three. The inclusive framework incorporates all three aspects: process, structure, and contents. Sustaining the paradoxical position among these three can free workers of the risk of inadvertently narrowing down their perceptions so much that they miss crucial groupwork needs.

GENUINE ACCOUNTABILITY

Much has been said and written about the need for accountability. Yet, this pressure for accountability can lead to questionable practices. It is quite possible to identify targets for change that do not do enough for the group members concerned. For example, understanding the cause and consequence of abusing power is very important. Yet, such an understanding on its own is very different from assimilating the experiences involved deeply enough so that change in the daily use of power follows. For mere understanding educational models of groupwork are sufficient. For change in daily life, more is needed. Periods of spontaneous expression of bewildering and sometimes even heavily censored experiences have to be allowed and even facilitated. Such personal experiences are not included in the educational model.

The present framework invited practitioners to account more fully for the approach they take with each group. By articulating the aspects that are expected to feature most clearly in each group, workers can explain the purpose of each in greater detail. Such explanations are helpful to members as they can choose whether the group is appropriate for them. Detailed explanations are also helpful for the workers as they can use supervision to more accurately clarify whether they are pursuing the group members' needs as best as they can. Fund holders are likely to benefit too as they can be realistic about the outcomes they can expect of each group. Last but by no means least: groupwork knowledge is likely to be enhanced when similarities and differences among many types of groups are explicitly formulated.

DYNAMIC COMPETENCE

In various disciplines of the helping professions the 'tick-box approach' to competence is rapidly established. In social work, practitioners have to show evidence that they can explain certain theories, adhere to certain moral values, and perform certain skills. In other disciplines the list may be somewhat different. In principle, the current approach to competence can easily become a recipe for a mechanistic assortment of abilities. As a result, the nature of the helping relationship as a whole can be easily lost.

Lest a misunderstanding arises, there is a great deal to be said for beginning to build up competence by rehearsing small and relatively well-documented steps. The inclusive stance does not preclude learning direct and linear interventions. Clearly, many of the interventions described under the umbrella term of 'stabilising' are valued step-by-step responses that workers can adopt.

The inclusive stance merely implies that more will eventually be required. Workers may well begin by learning each aspect separately. The problem may arise if they do not go further than that.

Linking skills, theory, and moral values to one another during each of the stages through which each group develops is only one aspect of dynamic competence. Another aspect is the ability to choose certain stages for a certain group while being mindful of the framework as a whole. To choose competently, workers will have to draw on a wider and deeper understanding of the relationships between clients' needs and group dynamics that may meet these needs.

Furthermore, such workers will have to appreciate the differences between phases and crises, and also the skills needed to facilitate each. Workers will need to identify turning points in the group's dynamics, and know how to sustain certain polarities. Yet, even these abilities may not be enough. By its own nature, the inclusive stance implies that not all the solutions are already spelled out in the inclusive blueprint. Working with some groups, workers may also have to be able to find new solutions by combining the aspects of group dynamics in ways that have not been identified in the inclusive blueprint.

All these abilities call for a rather different understanding of competence. Isolated bits and pieces of knowledge may not be enough to secure 'fitness of purpose' at this more advanced stage. The inclusive groupworker will have to be able to show how she manages inevitable tensions. These inevitable tensions may appear in many different ways: the tension between skills that separate interventions and theories that connect these responses is one challenge. The inevitable tension between working with only some of the stages while considering the framework of stages as a whole is another. Working within a given framework such as the inclusive blueprint while also innovating by evolving solutions that have not been spelled out by that framework is perhaps the most demanding venture.

Altogether, the emphasis on working with polarities may well lead to seeing competence as somewhat different from the established norm. What I call 'dynamic competence' may well be needed when groupworkers are fully committed to promoting awareness of group processes in pursuit of clients' needs.

FLEXIBILITY

When the dynamics sense of competence is accepted, the value of flexibility emerges even more clearly. Only very rarely would it seem helpful to automatically adopt recommended solutions. It seems far better to develop an inclusive understanding of group dynamics first. With these dynamics in mind, the worker can then develop relationships with group members to see how the various aspects of group dynamics may be combined to best meet their needs.

Yet, it is probably not very economic to start afresh every time a new group is set up. Some knowledge of groupwork practice has already accumulated – provisional as it may be. A good way of saving time and energy may be to draw on this knowledge first. Yet, drawing on existing knowledge is not the same as being enslaved to that body of documented experiences. It is quite possible to adopt certain ideas on a provisional basis and then revise these in the light of the emerging experience. I call this ability 'working with both hands'. On the one hand, the worker can have a pretty clear idea of where the group may go. Bearing in mind the agreed goal, it is possible to anticipate major needs and also some of the stages that may lead to meeting these needs. On the other hand, each worker can also just be there – entirely open to any unexpected experience as and when it emerges. During these 'empty moments' the worker does not plan, but improvises.

Indeed, there is tension between these opposites – of *planning* and *improvising*. The inclusive stance cherishes this tension and implies that learning to both plan and improvise should be part of being trained to work with groups. The inclusive groupworker works with both hands; continuously shuttling between these two modes.

INCLUSIVENESS

At the beginning of this book I raised the problem of eclectic fragmentation of groupwork. Each practitioner seems to adopt a framework that suits a particular situation. Some even adopt frameworks that were developed for meeting certain needs, while working with groups set up to meet quite different ones. The results prevent any comparison of various practices in groupwork and it is difficult to know how to improve practice. Faced with the forces of fragmentation, the temptation can be to integrate all practices into one. Integration means prescribing one framework that all workers follow. Yet, integration is not always as promising as it may appear. The trouble with integration is usually that it is short-lived. It is difficult and perhaps impossible to identify one and only one scheme of stages that will account sufficiently well for all the diverse needs served by groupwork already, and new needs may well emerge in the future. Desirable as it may be, *integration* is merely the opposite of *fragmentation*. Like other opposites it may well inevitably lead back to its counterpart; as needs and practice conditions change further, groupwork will fragment again.

The inclusive position avoids rigid integration. This position involves recognising the need to unearth the hidden context of working with groups. The hidden context surfaces when we become aware of communicating. When we focus on those moments of becoming aware of communicating we realise that we are living a paradox which I have called the paradox of talk. We can then learn to draw parallels to this paradox. By refining the art of drawing parallels we can, so to speak, have our cake and eat it. We can assimilate an inclusive blueprint of group stages without being enslaved into following all the stages all the time. Instead, we can adopt an evolving stance towards group stages. The evolving stance means that we do have an overall idea of the main possibilities, and out of these we evolve only those which may meet group members' needs best.

By its nature, such an evolving stance requires a higher level of abstraction compared to either pragmatic or prescribed frameworks. Indeed, increased freedom often incurs this price. The price of increased freedom to find our own choice is the commitment to be involved in working with somewhat more abstract ideas. Yet, of course groupwork is not abstract philosophy. As mentioned before, the point is to work with both hands. Thinking in a more abstract fashion has to be matched with more specific, concrete, and at times fuzzy experiences. Speaking from my limited experience, I can only say that after a while, working with both hands becomes quite natural, as long as genuine and honest relationships among people remain a priority.

As Martin Buber wrote:

> *And all that has frozen up and has become an object among objects, this is its essence and the mission treasured inside it – that it untie itself; return and untie from its migration.* (Buber 1963, p.30)

References

Agazarian, Y.M. (1997) *Systems-Centred Therapy for Groups*. New York: The Guilford Press.

Anderson, J. (1984) *Counselling the Group Process*. New York: Springer-Verlag.

Aveline, M. and Dryden, W. (eds) (1988) *Group Therapy in Britain*. Milton Keynes: Open University Press.

Bateson, G. (1971) *Steps to an Ecology of Mind*. New York: Ballantine Books.

Bateson, G. (1979) *Mind and Nature: A Necessary Unity*. Toronto: Bantam Books.

Bednar, R. and Kaul, T. (1994) 'Experiential group research.' In A.E. Bergin and S.L. Garfield (eds) *Handbook of Psychotherapy and Behavior Change (4th edn)*. *New York: John Wiley & Sons, 631–663*.

Benson, J.F. (1987) *Working more Creatively with Groups*. London: Tavistock Publishers.

Bernard, H.S. and MacKenzie, R. (eds) (1994) *Basics of Group Psychotherapy*. London: The Guilford Press.

Brammer, L.M., Abrego, P.J. and Shostrom, E.L. (1993) *Therapeutic Counselling and Psychotherapy* (6th edn). Englewood Cliffs, N.J.: Prentice Hall.

Brandler, S. and Roman, C.P. (1991) *Group Work: Skills and Strategies for Effective Interventions*. New York: The Howarth Press.

Breunlin, D.C. (1989) 'Clinical implications of oscillation theory: Family development and the process of change.' In C. Ramsey (ed) *The Science of Family Medicine*. New York: The Guilford Press, 135–149.

Brown, A. (1992) *Groupwork* (3rd edn). Aldershot: Ashgate.

Buber, M. (1963) *Philosophical Writings, Vol.I: In the Secret of Conversation*. Jerusalem: Byalik Institute. Translated from Hebrew by OM, with permission.

Butler, S. and Wintram, C. (1991) *Feminist Groupwork*. London: Sage.

Cohen, M.A. and Smith, R.D. (1971) *The Critical Incident Approach: Leadership Intervention in Small Groups*. Philadelphia: F.A. Davis Co.

Cohen, M.A. and Smith, R.D. (1972) 'The critical-incident approach to leadership intervention in training groups.' In W.G. Dyer (ed) *Modern Theory and Method in Group Training*. New York: Van Nostrand Reinhold Co., 84–106.

Corey, G., Corey, M. and Callanan, P. (1993) *Issues and Ethics in the Helping Professions* (4th edn). Pacific Groves, California: Brooks/Cole.

Corey, G., Corey, M.S., Callanan, P. and Russell, J.M. (1992) *Group Techniques* (2nd edn). Pacific Grove, California: Brooks/Cole.

Corey, G. (1995) *Group Counselling (4th edn). Pacific Grove, California: Brooks/Cole.*

Davis, L. and Proctor, E.K. (1989) *Race, Gender, and Class: Guidelines for Practice with Individuals, Families, and Groups.* Engelwood Cliffs, N.J.: Prentice Hall.

Doel, M. and Sawdon, C. (1999a) *The Essential Groupworker.* London: Jessica Kingsley.

Doel, M. and Sawdon, C. (1999b) 'No group is an island: groupwork in a social work agency.' *Groupwork 13,* 3 50–69.

Donigian, J. and Malnati, R. (1997) *Systemic Group Therapy: A Triadic Model.* Pacific Grove, California: Brooks/Cole.

Durkin, H.E. (1981) 'The technical implications of general systems theory for group psychotherapy.' In J. Durkin (ed) *Living Groups: Group Psychotherapy and General Systems Theory.* New York: Brunner/Mazel, 172–198.

Durkin, J.E. (ed) (1981) *Living Groups: Group Psychotherapy and General Systems Theory.* New York: Brunner/Mazel.

Flemons, D.G. (1991) *Completing Distinctions.* Boston: Shambala.

Foulkes, S.H. (1964) *Therapeutic Group Analysis.* New York: International Universities Press.

Fuhriman, A. and Burlingame, G.M. (1994) 'Measuring small group process: A methodological application of chaos theory.' *Small Group Research 25,* 4, 502–519.

Gemmill, G. and Wynkoop, C. (1991) 'The psychodynamics of small group transformation.' *Small Group Research 22,* 1, 4–23.

Gergen, K.J. (1982) *Towards Transformation in Social Knowledge.* New York: Springer-Verlag.

Gleick, J. (1987) *Chaos: Making a New Science.* London: Cardinal Sphere Books.

Gordon, D. (1978) *Therapeutic Metaphors.* Cupertino, California: META.

Hodge, J. (1977) 'Social groupwork: Rules for establishing the group.' *Social Work Today 8,* 7, 8–11.

Hodge, J. (1985) *Planning for Co-Leadership.* Newcastle upon Tyne: Groupvine.

Hoffman, L. (1981) *Foundations of Family Therapy.* New York: Basic Books.

Kantor, D. and Lehr, W. (1975) *Inside the Family.* London: Jossey-Bass.

Keeney, B.P. (1983) *Aesthetics of Change.* New York: The Guilford Press.

Kivlighan, D.M. and Goldfire, D.C. (1991) 'Endorsement of therapeutic factors as a function of stage of group development and participant interpersonal attitudes.' *Journal of Counseling Psychology 38,* 2, 150–158.

Kivlighan, D.M., Multon, K.D. and Brossart, D.F. (1996) 'Helpful impacts in group counseling: Development of multidimensional rating system.' *Journal of Counseling Psychology 43,* 3, 347–355.

Kivlighan, D.M. and Quigley, S.T. (1991) 'Dimensions used by experienced and novice group therapists to conceptualize group process.' *Journal of Counseling Psychology 38,* 4, 415–423.

Lacoursiere, R.B. (1980) *The Life Cycle of Groups.* New York: Human Science Press.

Leifer, R. (1989) 'Understanding organizational transformation using a dissipative structure model.' *Human Relations 42,* 10, 899–916.

Levine, B. (1979) *Group Psychotherapy: Practice and Development.* Englewood Cliffs, N.J.: Prentice Hall.

MacKenzie, K.R. (1997) *Time-Managed Group Psychotherapy.* Washington DC: American Psychiatric Press.

Malekoff, A. (1997) *Group Work with Adolescents.* London: The Guilford Press.

Manor, O. (ed) (1984) *Family Work in Action: A Handbook for Social Workers.* London: Tavistock.

Manor, O. (1986) 'The preliminary interview in social group work: Finding the spiral steps.' *Social Work with Groups 9,* 20, 21–39.

Manor, O. (1988) 'Preparing the client for social group work: An illustrated framework.' *Groupwork 1,* 2, 100–114.

Manor, O. (1989) 'Organising accountability in social groupwork: More choices.' *Groupwork 2,* 2, 108–122.

Manor, O. (1992) 'Transactional analysis, object relations, and the systems approach: Finding the counterparts.' *Transactional Analysis Journal 22,* 1, 4–15.

Manor, O. (1994) 'Group psychotherapy.' In P. Clarkson and M. Pokorney (eds) *The Handbook of Psychotherapy.* London: Routledge, 249–264.

Manor, O. and Dumbleton, M. (1993) 'Combining activities and growth games: A systems approach.' *Groupwork 6,* 3, 248–265.

Manor, O. (1997) 'Storming as transformation: A case study of group relationships.' *Groupwork 9,* 3, 259–282.

McClure, B.A. (1998) *Putting a New Spin on Groups: The Science of Chaos.* London: Lawrence Erlbaum Associates.

Middleman, R.R. and Goldberg Wood, G. (1990) *Skills for Direct Practice in Social Work.* New York: Columbia University Press.

Mistry, T. and Brown, A. (eds) (1997) *Race and Groupwork.* London: Whiting and Birch.

Mullender, A. and Ward, D. (1991) *Self-Directed Groupwork.* London: Whiting and Birch.

O'Hara, G. (1988) 'Preparing families in groups.' In J. Triseliotis (ed) *Groupwork in Adoption and Foster Care.* London: B.T. Batsford, 40–56.

Parkes, C.M. (1986) *Bereavement: Studies of Grief in Adult Life* (2nd edn). London: Penguin Books.

Pawlak, E.J. and LeCroy, C.W. (1981) 'Critical incident recording for supervision and treatment in group practice.' *Social Work with Groups 4,* 1/2, 181–191.

Peile, C. (1994) *The Creative Paradigm.* Aldershot: Avebury.

Perls, F., Hefferline, R.F. and Goodman, P.G. (1951) *Gestalt Therapy.* New York: Delta Press.

Pinsof, W.M. (1994) 'An integrative systems perspective on the therapeutic alliance: Theoretical, clinical, and research implications.' In A.O. Hovarth and L.S. Greenberg (eds) *The Working Alliance: Theory, Research, and Practice.* New York: John Wiley & Sons, 173–195.

Ponze, Z. (1991) 'Critical factors in group work.' *Journal for Specialists in Group Work 16,* 1, 16–23.

Prigogine, I. and Stengers, I. (1984) *Order out of Chaos: Man's New Dialogue with Nature.* London: Fontana Paperbacks.

Rogers, C.R. and Skinner, B.F. (1956) 'Some issues concerning the control of human behavior.' *Science 124*, 1057–1066.

Rogers, C.R. (1970) *Encounter Groups*. London: Allen Lane, The Penguin Press.

Rohde, R.I. and Stockton, R. (1994) 'Group structure: A review.' *Journal of Group Psychotherapy, Psychodrama, and Sociometry 46*, 4, 151–158.

Rose, S. and Edleson, J. (1987) *Working with Children and Adolescents in Groups*. San Francisco: Jossey-Bass.

Rosenbaum, R.L. (1982) 'Paradox as epistemological jump.' *Family Process 21*, 85–89.

Simon, F.B., Stierlin, H. and Wynne, L.C. (1985) *The Language of Family Therapy*. New York: The Family Process Press.

Sluzki, C.E. (1983) 'Process, structure and world views: Towards an integrated view of systems models in family therapy.' *Family Process 22*, 4, 469–476.

Smith, K.K. and Berg, D.N. (1987) *Paradoxes of Group Life*. San Francisco: Jossey-Bass.

Speed, B. (1991) 'Reality exists O.K.? An argument against constructivism and constructionism.' *Journal of Family Therapy 13*, 4, 395–409.

Stockton, R., Rohde, R.I. and Haughey, J. (1992) 'The effects of structured group exercises on cohesion, engagement, avoidance, and conflict.' *Small Group Research 23*, 2, 155–168.

Stroebe, M. (1992–3) 'Coping with bereavement: A review of the grief work hypothesis.' *Omega 26*, 1, 19–24.

Sue, D.W. and Sue, D. (1990) *Counselling the Culturally Different: Theory and Practice (2nd edn). New York: Wiley.*

Toseland, R.W. and Rivas, R.F. (1984) *An Introduction to Group Work Practice*. London: Collier MacMillan.

Toseland, R.W. (1990) *Groupwork with Older Adults*. New York: New York University Press.

Tuckman, B.W. and Jensen, M.A. (1977) 'Stages of small group development revisited.' *Group and Organizational Studies 2*, 419–427.

Tudor, K. (1999) *Group Counselling*. London: Sage.

Vasco, A.B. and Dryden, W. (1994) 'The development of psychotherapists' theoretical orientation and clinical practice.' *British Journal of Guidance and Counselling 22*, 3, 327–341.

Walters, T. (1996) 'A new model of grief: Bereavement and biography'. *Mortality 1*, 1, 7–25.

Wilden, A. (1980) *System and Structure* (2nd edn). London: Tavistock.

Winnicott, D.W. (1971) *Playing and Reality*. London: Tavistock.

Worden, J.W. (1983) *Grief Counselling and Grief Therapy*. London: Tavistock.

Yalom, I.D. (1995) *The Theory and Practice of Group Psychotherapy* (4th edn). New York: Basic Books.

Subject Index

Author Index